I0555206

My Book

This book belongs to

*Name:*_____

©All rights reserved-Math-Knots LLC., VA-USA
www.math-knots.com

Copy right © 2019 MATH-KNOTS LLC

All rights reserved, no part of this publication may be reproduced, stored in any system or transmitted in any form, or by any means, electronic, mechanical, photocopying, recording, or otherwise without the written permission of MATH-KNOTS LLC.

Cover Design by :
MATH-KNOTS LLC

First Edition :
January, 2019

Author:
Gowri Vemuri

Questions: mathknots.help@gmail.com

* CogAT® and Cognitive Abilities Test ® are registered trademarks of Riverside Publishing company

(A Houghton Mifflin Harcourt company) is neither affiliated, nor sponsors or endorses this product.

This book is dedicated to:

My Mom, who is my best critic, guide and supporter.

To what I am today, and what I am going to become tomorrow,

is all because of your blessings, unconditional affection and support.

This book is dedicated to the

strongest women of my life ,

my dearest mom

and

to all those moms in this universe.

G.V.

©All rights reserved-Math-Knots LLC., VA-USA

What is CogAT ?

The Cognitive Ability Test® (CogAT) test measures thinking and analytical skills in young children from K-12, in various sections of Verbal, Quantitative and Non-Verbal. Many counties and states conduct this test to identify kids for CogAT serves as one of the basic measures to identify the Gifted and Talented pool for accelerated educational programs in many counties and states.

Cognitive skills are the skills the brain uses to think, learn, read, remember, pay attention, and solve problems. Kids develop these skills as part of their growing up. Our book helps kids, in channelizing their skills.

As Einstein said "Education is not the learning of facts, but the training of minds to think". We want to bring joy of learning while channelizing the young minds thinking to reach their optimum potential. Students get familiarized with various strategies, tips and techniques thus improving their thinking abilities. All our tests are created in a multi-color, kid friendly format. For each test is based on theme for the students to have a little fun as they learn. As the students get familiarize with testing format, their vocabulary also builds up.

Our tests give an edge and simulate the testing pattern, in such a way that child feels very comfortable when they take the test in their schools.

Various counties and states apply multiple criteria for selecting kids for gifted or Advanced Academic programs and CogAT is one of the basic criteria. CogAT comprises of the following three main categories

- Verbal Section
- Quantitative Aptitude
- Non-Verbal Section.

Our Practice tests are based on the following:

Verbal Section:

Students are tested in the areas of vocabulary, comprehension of ideas, and the relation between various words. The test comprises of the below three sub sections/tests.

1. **Verbal Classification**

Three words that are alike in some way and form a group are given to the students, along with four choices to choose. One of the four choices don't belong to the group. Student has to identify the odd man and bubbles the correct option in the bubble sheet.

2. Sentence Completion

A sentence is given to the student with four picture options. Student uses the vocabulary and comprehension skills and choses the right picture that makes the best sense in the sentence. Student bubbles the correct option in the bubble sheet.

3. Verbal Analogies

The student is given three words. The first two words go together. The third word goes with one of the answer choices. The student is asked to choose the word that goes with the third word the same way that the second word goes with the first. Student bubbles the correct option in the bubble sheet.

Quantitative Aptitude Section:

The Quantitative Aptitude sub sections tests the student's abstract reasoning, quantitative reasoning, analytical and problem-solving skills. The test comprises of the below three sub sections/tests.

1. Quantitative Relations/Number Analogies

Figures in the first row belong to each other in a certain way. Student is expected to identify the number analogy in the first row. The figures in the second row follow the same analogy as the first row. Student analyzes and thinks through to find the right choice from the given four options. Student bubbles the correct option in the bubble sheet.

2. Number Series

Series of beads are given on various strings /rods. Student identifies the number series and figures out the beads on missing rod/string. Student bubbles the correct option in the bubble sheet.

3. Equation Building /Number Puzzles

A number equation is given in a kid friendly format. Student solves for the number that goes in the place of the question mark. Student bubbles the correct option in the bubble sheet.

Non-Verbal Section (Spatial Reasoning):

The Nonverbal Battery comprises of the most unique problems to students. The questions on these tests are based on geometric shapes and figures. The tests require visualization, thinking and analytical abilities. The test comprises of the below three sub tests.

1.   Figure Classification

The student is given three figures that are a like in some way. Four answer choices are given to choose from and one of the choices belong to the given group in a certain way. Students analyzes the figures to choose the right option and bubbles the correct option in the bubble sheet.

2.   Figure Analogies/ Figure Matrices

Figures in the first row belong to each other in a certain way. Student is expected to identify the figure analogy between figures in the first row. The figures in the second row follow the same analogy as the first row. Student analyzes and thinks through to find the right choice from the given four options and bubbles the correct option in the bubble sheet.

3.   Figure Analysis/Paper Folding

A Square, Rectangle or any shape figure is folded once or more as shown in the figure. Holes are punched to the folded figure and opened completely. Students are expected to think through on how the figure will look like after opening it up and bubbles the correct option in the bubble sheet.

Book Includes, detailed solutions and tips, that will help kids do well in the **CogAT test.**

Do Visit our website www.math-knots.com for more products and also for our online subscription.

Math-Knots ------- Joy of Learning

INDEX

©All rights reserved-Math-Knots LLC., VA-USA

www.math-knots.com

INDEX

©All rights reserved-Math-Knots LLC., VA-USA

www.math-knots.com

Start from the middle of right choice and fully fill the bubble completely.

Wrong

A   B ◯   C ◯   D ◯

Wrong

A ◯   B ◯   C   D ◯

Wrong

A ◯   B ◯   C   D ◯

Partial Filled Bubble is not correct.

Correct

A ◯   B ◯   C ●   D ◯

©All rights reserved-Math-Knots LLC., VA-USA

PREPARATION FOR THE TEST

1. To simulate the testing format, a parent or an adult shall read the questions to the student to answer the practice test sets.

2. Student need to have a pencil and an eraser.

3. Student need to make sure they are bubbling the circles in the right way.

Before the testing date.

1. Make sure the child has a good nights sleep and a good breakfast.

©All rights reserved-Math-Knots LLC., VA-USA

www.math-knots.com

©All rights reserved-Math-Knots LLC., VA-USA

TEST - 1

VERBAL SECTION

VERBAL CLASSIFICATION

Lets Start the Test...

©All rights reserved-Math-Knots LLC., VA-USA

www.math-knots.com

©All rights reserved-Math-Knots LLC., VA-USA

www.math-knots.com

Sample   Three words are related in a certain way. Four options are given. Identify the choice that does not belong to the group ?

One	Two	Three	
Six	Eight	Five	Gate
A ◯	B ◯	C ◯	D ◯

Solution : D

Three words in the question belong to one group. One of the four choices doesn't belong to the same group. Identify and bubble the correct choice. In the given question all three in first row are words as well as numbers in words. Lets take a look at the answers. All choices are words but three are numbers in words and one other word gate, which is incorrect.

©All rights reserved-Math-Knots LLC., VA-USA

All the questions in verbal classification test 1 are to be answered following the below question (instruction).

Three words are related in a certain way. Four options are given. Identify the choice that <u>does not belong</u> to the group ?

1. **Dress**   **Shorts**   **Tie**

   Umbrella   Pant   Socks   Shirt

   A ◯   B ◯   C ◯   D ◯

2. **Earthquakes**   **Hurricane**   **Catastrophe**

   War   Tornado   Blizzard   Floods

   A ◯   B ◯   C ◯   D ◯

3. **Yellow**   **Orange**   **Green**

   Red   Blue   Color   Orange

   A ◯   B ◯   C ◯   D ◯

4. **Eyes**   **Nose**   **Hearing**

   Skin   Tongue   Sound   Teeth

   A ◯   B ◯   C ◯   D ◯

5. **Nitrogen**   **Helium**   **Oxygen**

   Carbon dioxide   Zone   Hydrogen   Ozone

   A ◯   B ◯   C ◯   D ◯

6. **Awesome**   **Fantastic**   **Happy**

   Lively   Ecstatic   Joy   Gloomy

   A ◯   B ◯   C ◯   D ◯

7. **Gold**   **Bronze**   **Iron**

   Mercury   Copper   Steel   Tin

   A ◯   B ◯   C ◯   D ◯

8. **Shoulder**   **Hip**   **Fingers**

   Knee   Palm   Ankle   Elbow

   A ◯   B ◯   C ◯   D ◯

9. **Lawyer**   **Professor**   **Doctor**

   Engineer   Fire Fighter   Journalist   Learner

   A ◯   B ◯   C ◯   D ◯

10. **Mentor**   **Coach**   **Principal**

   Professor   Teacher   Student   Tutor

   A ◯   B ◯   C ◯   D ◯

11. **Viola**   **Guitar**   **Sitar**

Violin   Tabla   Cello   Harp

A ◯   B ◯   C ◯   D ◯

12. **Creek**   **River**   **Brook**

Runnel   Pond   Stream   Spring

A ◯   B ◯   C ◯   D ◯

13. **Twig**   **Branch**   **Flower**

Trunk   Tree   Fruit   Root

A ◯   B ◯   C ◯   D ◯

14. **Train**   **Helicopter**   **Bus**

Transport   Airplane   Cab   Ferry

A ◯   B ◯   C ◯   D ◯

15. **Skiers**   **Wrestler**   **Jockey**

Archers   Boxers   Player   Rowers

A ◯   B ◯   C ◯   D ◯

16. **Freedom**   **Admission**   **Sanction**

Permit   Agree   Consent   Confess

A ◯   B ◯   C ◯   D ◯

17. **Fence**   **Door**   **Desk**

Firewood   Wood   Tooth Picks   Deck

A ◯   B ◯   C ◯   D ◯

18. **Climax**   **Vertex**   **Zenith**

Pack   Acme   Crest   Peak

A ◯   B ◯   C ◯   D ◯

TEST - 1

VERBAL SECTION

SENTENCE COMPLETION

Lets Start the Test...

©All rights reserved-Math-Knots LLC., VA-USA

www.math-knots.com

©All rights reserved-Math-Knots LLC., VA-USA

Sample

Look at the question with the Tennis Ball. Maya is trying to solve the below brain teaser. "Rik has more stamps then Ryan. Ryan has more stamps than Luke. Who has more stamps?" Bubble the correct option.

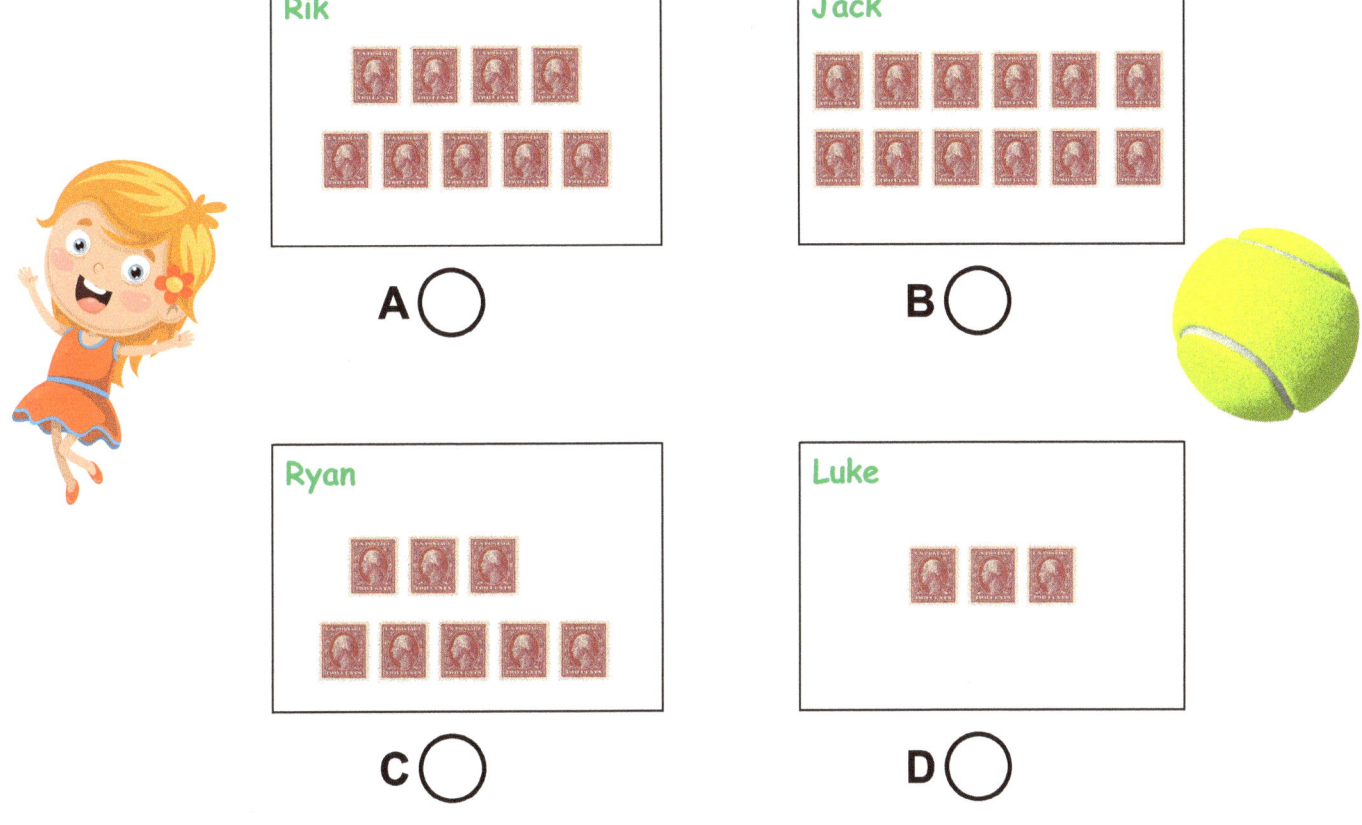

Solution : A

The Correct choice is A. The question doesn't compare with what Jack has.

Rik has the most stamps.

Rik >   Ryan >   Luke

©All rights reserved-Math-Knots LLC., VA-USA

Q-1

Look at the question with the Ice Cream. Ben and Fred are at a camping site. They together made a tent and are looking at it. A strong wing blew. What could have happened to the tent? Identify the correct picture and help them to bubble the correct option.

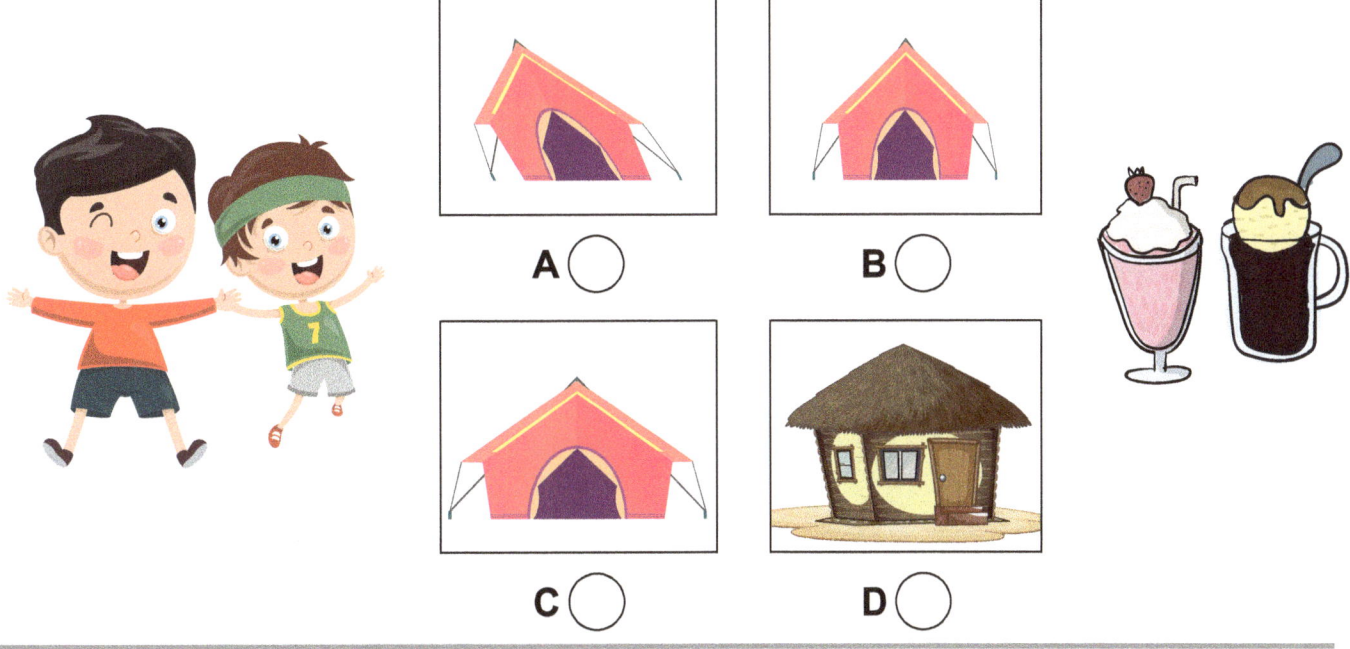

A ◯   B ◯

C ◯   D ◯

Q-2

Look at the question with the Bread. Mrs. Kim's father lives thousands of miles away and is admitted in hospital. She wants to visit her father. Which is the fastest way to travel? Identify the correct picture from the given choices below. Help her to bubble the correct option.

A ◯   B ◯

C ◯   D ◯

©All rights reserved-Math-Knots LLC., VA-USA

Q-3

Look at the question with the Milk Bottle. Liam wants to cross the river and reach the other shore. Help him to choose the right transportation from the below choices. Bubble the correct option.

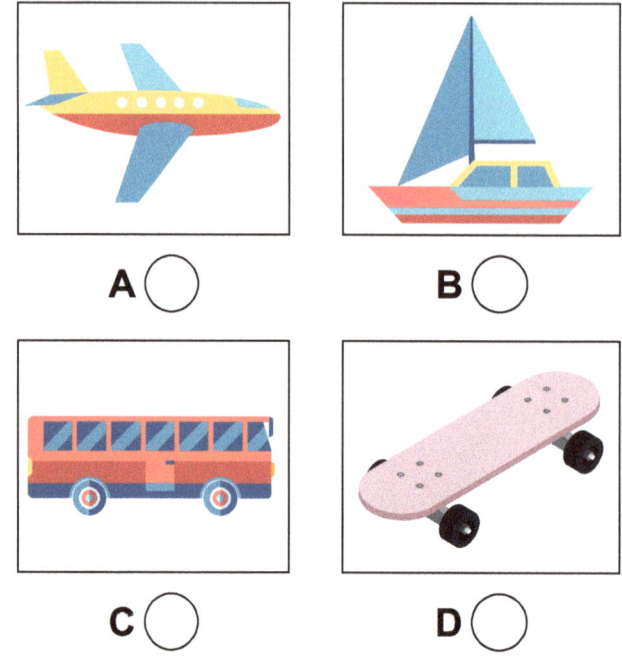

A ○   B ○

C ○   D ○

Q-4

Look at the question with the Coffee Mug. Lucy wants to go out for shopping in her new car. What do you think she should take with her along from the below choices? Bubble the correct option.

A ○   B ○

C ○   D ○

©All rights reserved-Math-Knots LLC., VA-USA

www.math-knots.com

Q-5 Look at the question with the Muffin. Schools have a snow day off today. Rita wants to go out and play in snow. What do you think she shall choose from the below choices? Bubble the correct option.

A ◯   B ◯

C ◯   D ◯

Q-6 Look at the question with the Jell-O. While Emily is reading a book, she comes across the word "Enclosed". She wondering what not enclosed means? What do you think she shall choose from the below choices? Bubble the correct option.

A ◯   B ◯

C ◯   D ◯

©All rights reserved-Math-Knots LLC., VA-USA
www.math-knots.com

Q-7

Look at the question with the Oil Jar. Noah is trying to find a single object? What do you think he shall choose from the below choices? Bubble the correct option.

A ◯   B ◯

C ◯   D ◯

Q-8

Look at the question with the French Fries. Henry is trying to find the nine planets? What do you think he shall choose from the below choices? Bubble the correct option.

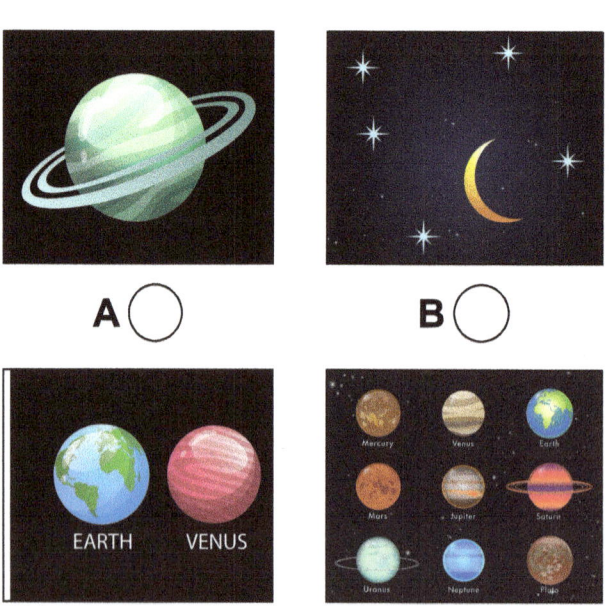

A ◯   B ◯

C ◯   D ◯

©All rights reserved-Math-Knots LLC., VA-USA

www.math-knots.com

Q-9

Look at the question with the House. Raksha is trying to find which of the below can Fly? What do you think she shall choose from the below choices? Bubble the correct option.

A ◯

B ◯

C ◯

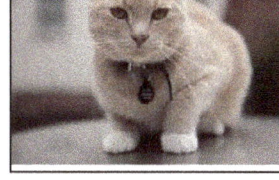
D ◯

Q-10

Look at the question with the Turkey. Aiden is trying to find three pairs of objects? What do you think he shall choose from the below choices? Bubble the correct option.

A ◯

B ◯

C ◯

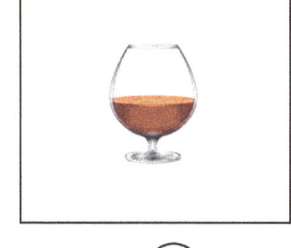
D ◯

©All rights reserved-Math-Knots LLC., VA-USA

www.math-knots.com

Q-11

Look at the question with the Cake. Carl wants to charge his cell phone and laptop? What do you think he shall choose from the below choices? Bubble the correct option.

A ◯

B ◯

C ◯

D ◯

Q-12

Look at the question with the Tea Kettle. Aria is looking around for her hair band. What do you think she shall choose from the below choices? Bubble the correct option.

A ◯

B ◯

C ◯

D ◯

©All rights reserved-Math-Knots LLC., VA-USA

www.math-knots.com

Q-13

Look at the question with the Pan Cakes. Xavier wants to know the meaning of pack. What do you think he shall choose from the below choices resembling pack? Bubble the correct option.

A ◯   B ◯

C ◯   D ◯

Q-14

Look at the question with the Bread Toast. Rosy bought a Soccer Post and wanted to fix it immediately for her kids to play. She is looking into her tool box. What do you think she will find in her tool box from the choices below? Bubble the correct option.

A ◯   B ◯

C ◯   D ◯

©All rights reserved-Math-Knots LLC., VA-USA

www.math-knots.com

Q-15 Look at the question with the Sandwich. Karen is sitting in the garden and hears a croak sound. Which of the below choices made the sound? Bubble the correct option.

A ◯   B ◯

C ◯   D ◯

Q-16 Look at the question with the Soup Bowl. Sriyan, who is turning one year soon is playing with toys. Which of the below choices will he have trouble opeing? Bubble the correct option.

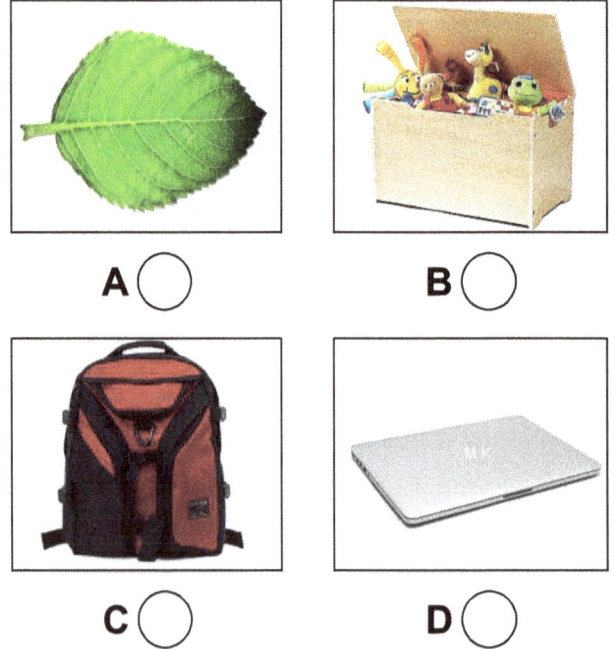

A ◯   B ◯

C ◯   D ◯

©All rights reserved-Math-Knots LLC., VA-USA

www.math-knots.com

Q-17 Look at the question with the Ketchup Bottle. Ian is a member of his high school strings club. He goes to the music store to buy a new instrument. Which of the below could be his choice? Bubble the correct option.

A ◯   B ◯

C ◯   D ◯

Q-18 Look at the question with the Fried eggs. Samantha knows that Tomatoes are red in color. She is wondering which of the below choices are of the same color. Help her bubble the correct option.

A ◯   B ◯

C ◯   D ◯

©All rights reserved-Math-Knots LLC., VA-USA   www.math-knots.com

©All rights reserved-Math-Knots LLC., VA-USA

www.math-knots.com

TEST - 1

VERBAL SECTION

VERBAL ANALOGIES

Lets Start the Test...

©All rights reserved-Math-Knots LLC., VA-USA

©All rights reserved-Math-Knots LLC., VA-USA

Sample   The first two words are related in a certain way as the next two words. Identify the missing word.

Clouds : White :: Sky : ?

Bold   Blue   Silver   Yellow

A ◯   B ◯   C ◯   D ◯

Solution : B

First analogy is color of the clouds which is white. Color of sky is blue.

Right choice is B.

Student needs to think through how the first two are related and then relate it to next analogy in the same way. Bubble the correct option.

©All rights reserved-Math-Knots LLC., VA-USA

All the questions in verbal analogies test 1 are to be answered following the below question (instruction).

The first two words are related in a certain way as the next two words. <u>Identify the missing word.</u>

©All rights reserved-Math-Knots LLC., VA-USA

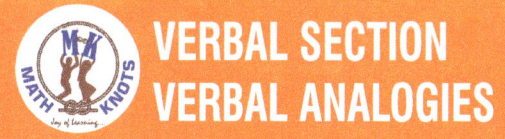
1.   Ship : Water :: Airplane :   ?

   Sky   Road   Travel   Gate

   A◯   B◯   C◯   D◯

2.   Deer : Grass lands :: Bull : ?

   Den   Kennel   Stable   Cattle Shed

   A◯   B◯   C◯   D◯

3.   Hand : Fingers :: ? : Toes

   Ankle   Knee   Feet   Arm

   A◯   B◯   C◯   D◯

4.   Ocean : Surfing :: Sand :   ?

   Soccer Ball   Basket Ball   Bricks   Castles

   A◯   B◯   C◯   D◯

5.   Trees : Green :: Sky :   ?

   Blue   Plane   Clouds   Rain

   A◯   B◯   C◯   D◯

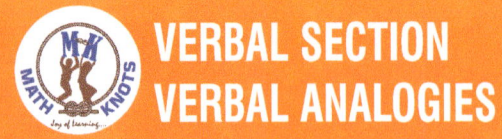
6. **Shorts : Summer :: Fur Coat : ?**

    Miami   Spring   Winter   Snow man

    A ◯   B ◯   C ◯   D ◯

7. **Summer : June :: Spring : ?**

    April   June   September   December

    A ◯   B ◯   C ◯   D ◯

8. **Mosquito : Blood :: Termites : ?**

    Bees   Metal   Leaves   Wood

    A ◯   B ◯   C ◯   D ◯

9. **Numbers : Math :: Alphabets : ?**

    Vowels   Consonants   Reading   Briley

    A ◯   B ◯   C ◯   D ◯

10. **Camera : Pictures :: Paintbrush : ?**

    Pixel   Painting   Draw   Frame

    A ◯   B ◯   C ◯   D ◯

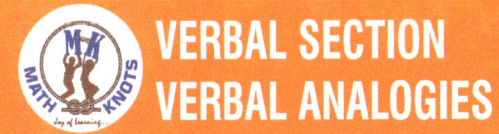

11.   **Spring : Leaves Grow :: Fall : ?**

Leaves   Flowers Bloom   Harvesting   Leaves Fall

A◯   B◯   C◯   D◯

12.   **Sun : Day :: Moon :   ?**

Night   Afternoon   Dusk   Morning

A◯   B◯   C◯   D◯

13.   **Owl : Owlet :: Deer : ?**

Calf   Moan   Fawn   Cub

A◯   B◯   C◯   D◯

14.   **Solo : One :: Duet : ?**

Five   Two   Triplet   One

A◯   B◯   C◯   D◯

15.   **Echinoderms : 5 legs :: Deco pods :   ?**

Six legs   Four legs   Two legs   Ten legs

A◯   B◯   C◯   D◯

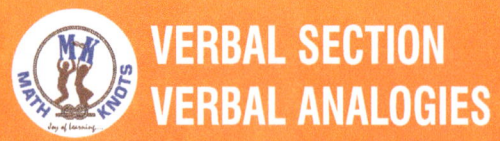
16.   Bank : Money :: Library : ?

Computers   Books   Food   Service

A ◯   B ◯   C ◯   D ◯

17.   Bury : Cover :: Dig : ?

Hide   Open   Uncover   Close

A ◯   B ◯   C ◯   D ◯

18.   Decade : 10 Years :: Century : ?

One Hundred Years   A ◯

One Million Years   B ◯

Five Hundred Years   C ◯

Thousand years   D ◯

©All rights reserved-Math-Knots LLC., VA-USA
www.math-knots.com

TEST - 1

QUANTITATIVE APTITUDE

NUMBER ANALOGIES

Lets Start the Test...

©All rights reserved-Math-Knots LLC., VA-USA

www.math-knots.com

©All rights reserved-Math-Knots LLC., VA-USA

Sample Look at the question with the Parrot. Two boxes in the first row are related in a certain way which is similar to two boxes in the second row. Ken is trying to fill the bubble under the correct option. Help him to select from options A, B, C, and D.

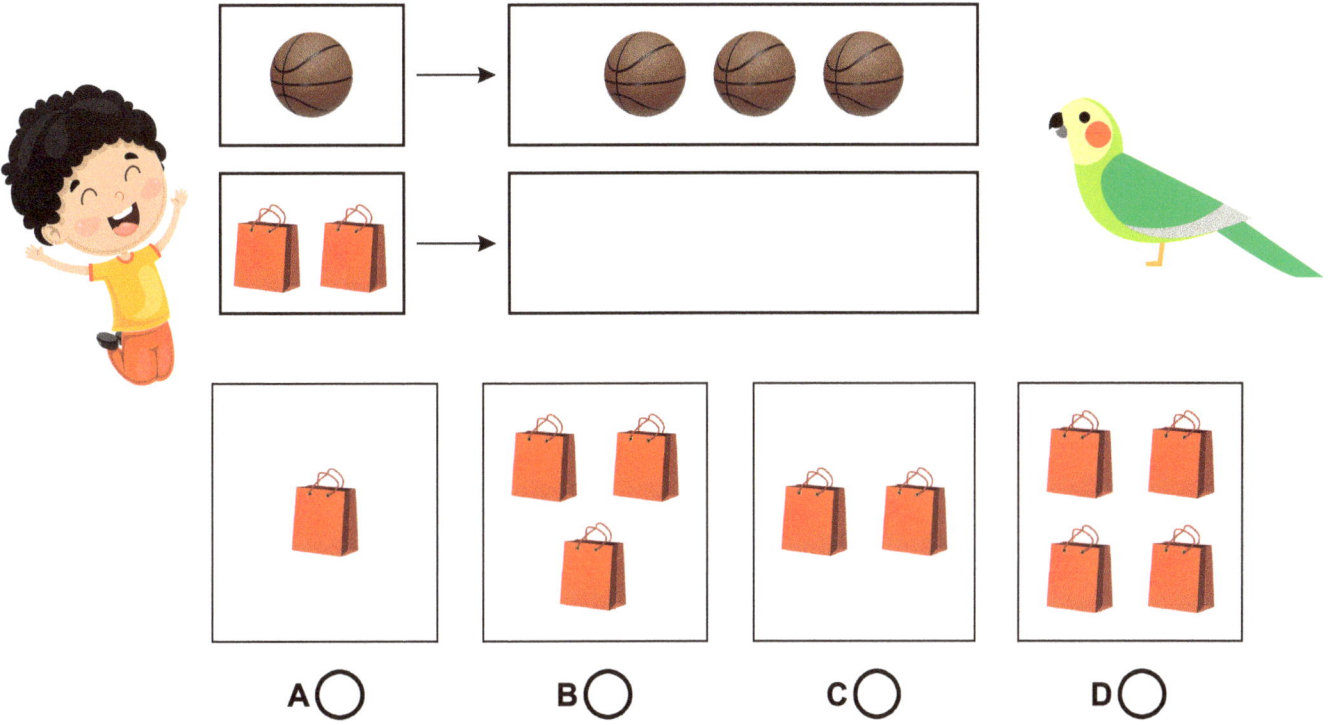

A ○   B ○   C ○   D ○

Solution : D

In first row, one ball to three balls [(1+2) adding two more]

In second row, two bags by adding two more will become four bags.

The analogies can be formed by adding or subtracting a certain number meaning increasing or decreasing by a certain quantity. Students needs to understand the right analogy and bubble the correct option.

©All rights reserved-Math-Knots LLC., VA-USA

Q-1 Look at the question with the Soccer Ball. Two boxes in the first row are related in a certain way which is similar to two boxes in the second row. Sam is trying to fill the bubble under the correct option. Help him to select from options A, B, C, and D.

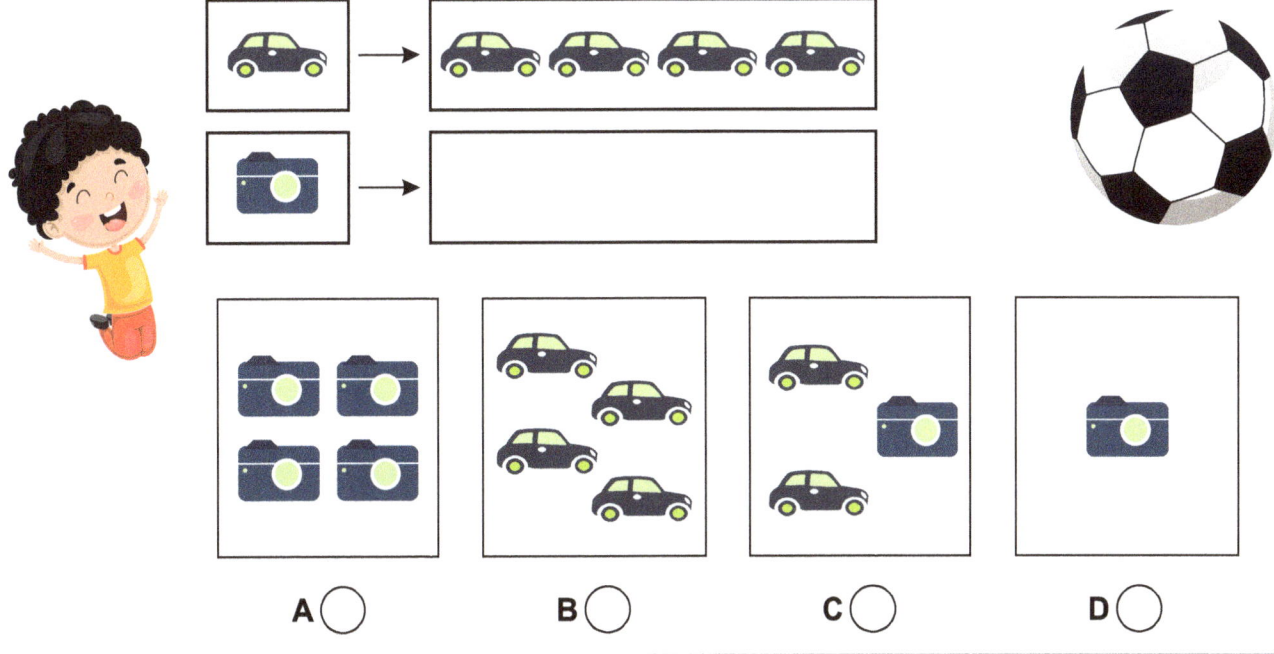

Q-2 Look at the question with the Foot Ball. Two boxes in the first row are related in a certain way which is similar to two boxes in the second row. Mary is trying to to fill the bubble under the correct option. Help her to select from options A, B, C, and D.

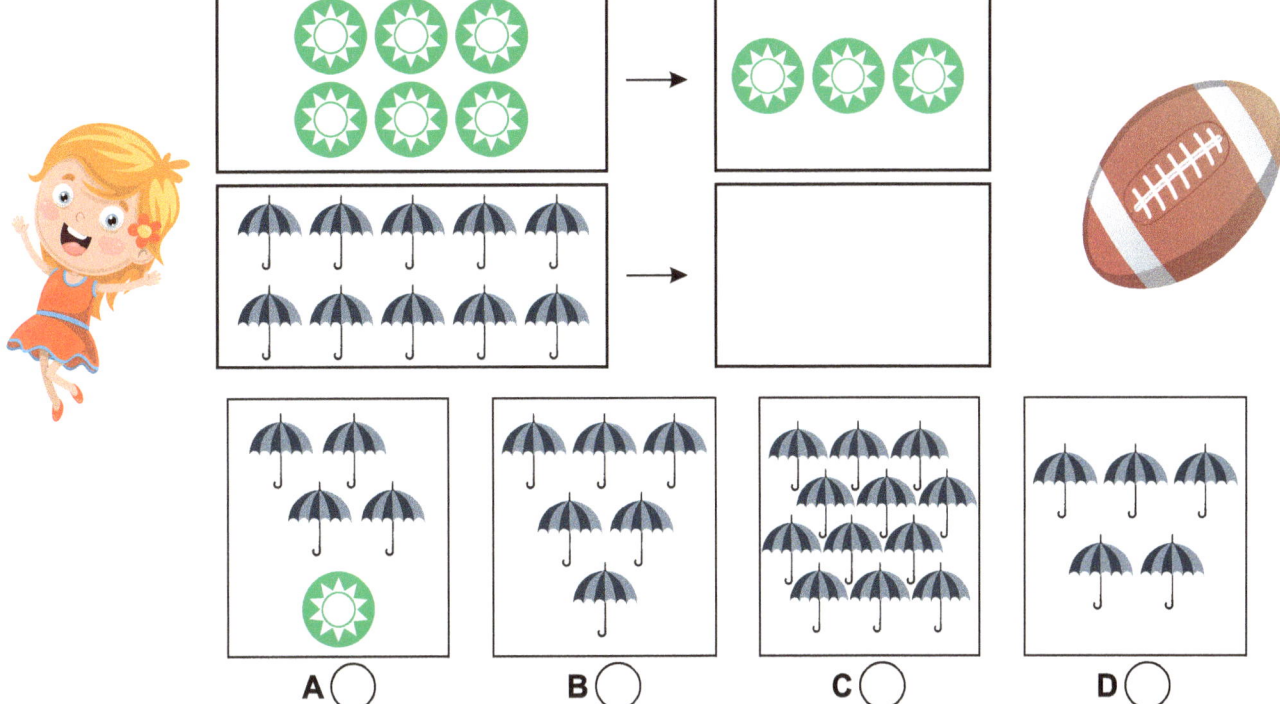

Q-3

Look at the question with the Basket Ball. Two boxes in the first row are related in a certain way which is similar to two boxes in the second row. Sri is trying to fill the bubble under the correct option. Help her to select from options A, B, C, and D.

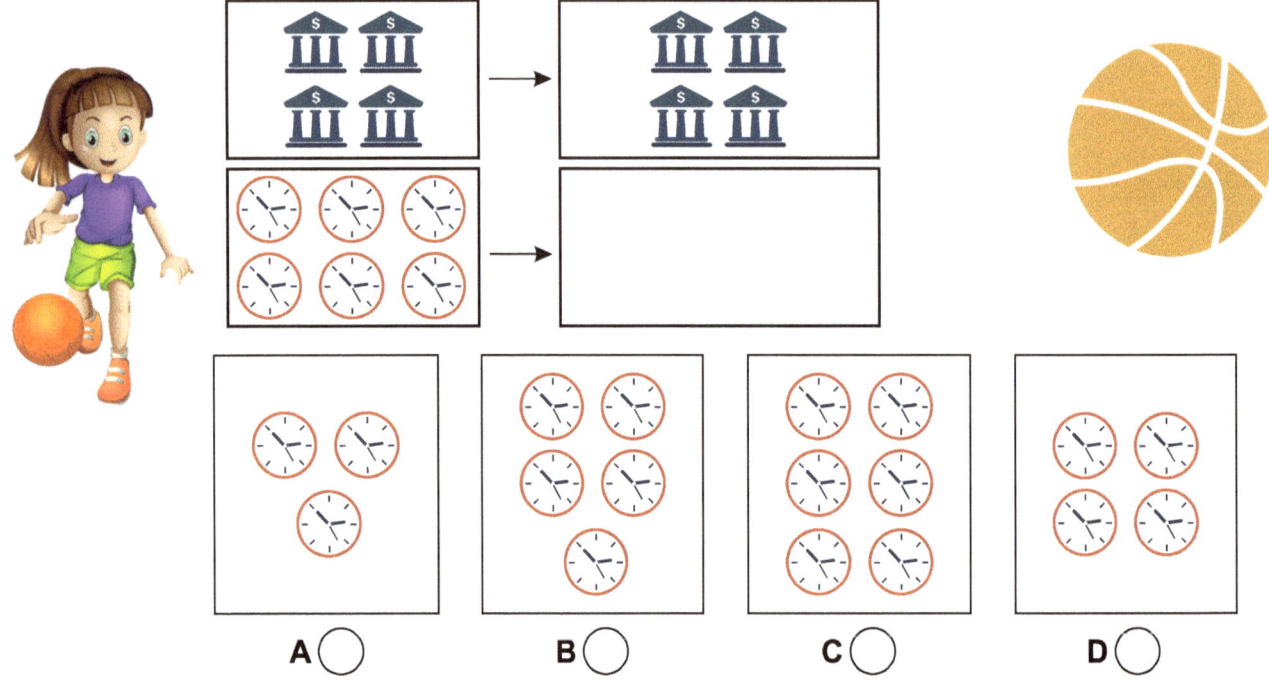

A ◯   B ◯   C ◯   D ◯

Q-4

Look at the question with the Shuttlecock. Two boxes in the first row are related in a certain way which is similar to two boxes in the second row. Robert is trying to fill the bubble under the correct option. Help him to select from options A, B, C, and D.

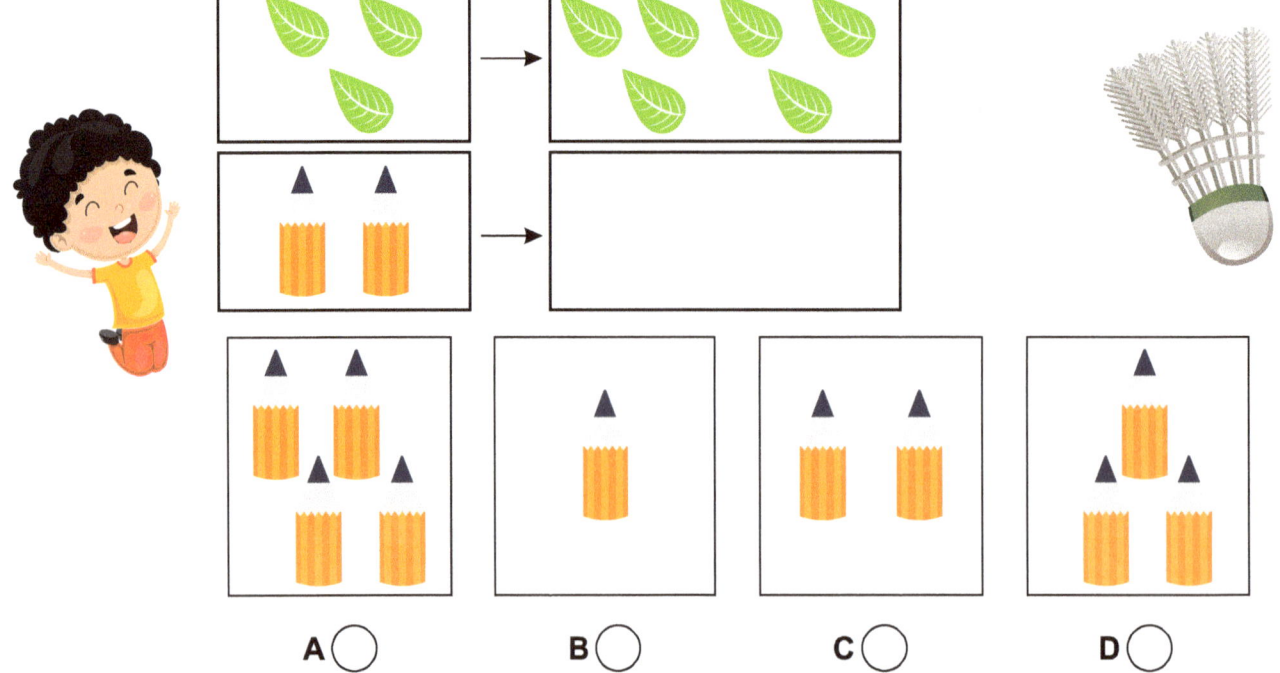

A ◯   B ◯   C ◯   D ◯

©All rights reserved-Math-Knots LLC., VA-USA
www.math-knots.com

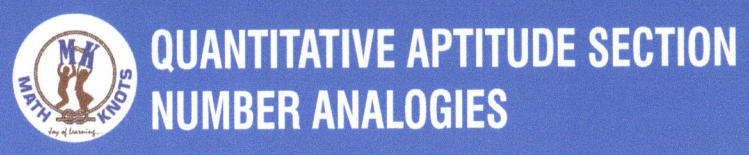

Q-5 Look at the question with the Bowling Pin. Two boxes in the first row are related in a certain way which is similar to two boxes in the second row. Sreya is trying to fill the bubble under the correct option. Help her to select from options A, B, C, and D.

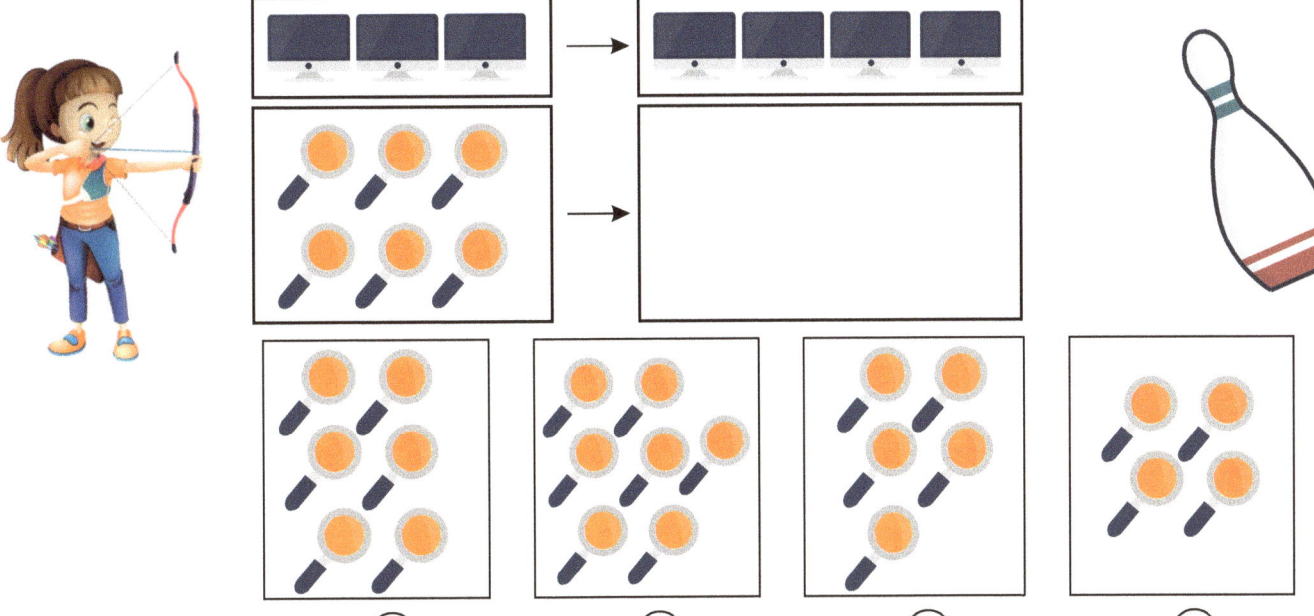

A ◯   B ◯   C ◯   D ◯

Q-6 Look at the question with the Hockey Stick. Two boxes in the first row are related in a certain way which is similar to two boxes in the second row. Sofia is trying to fill the bubble under the correct option. Help her to select from options A, B, C, and D.

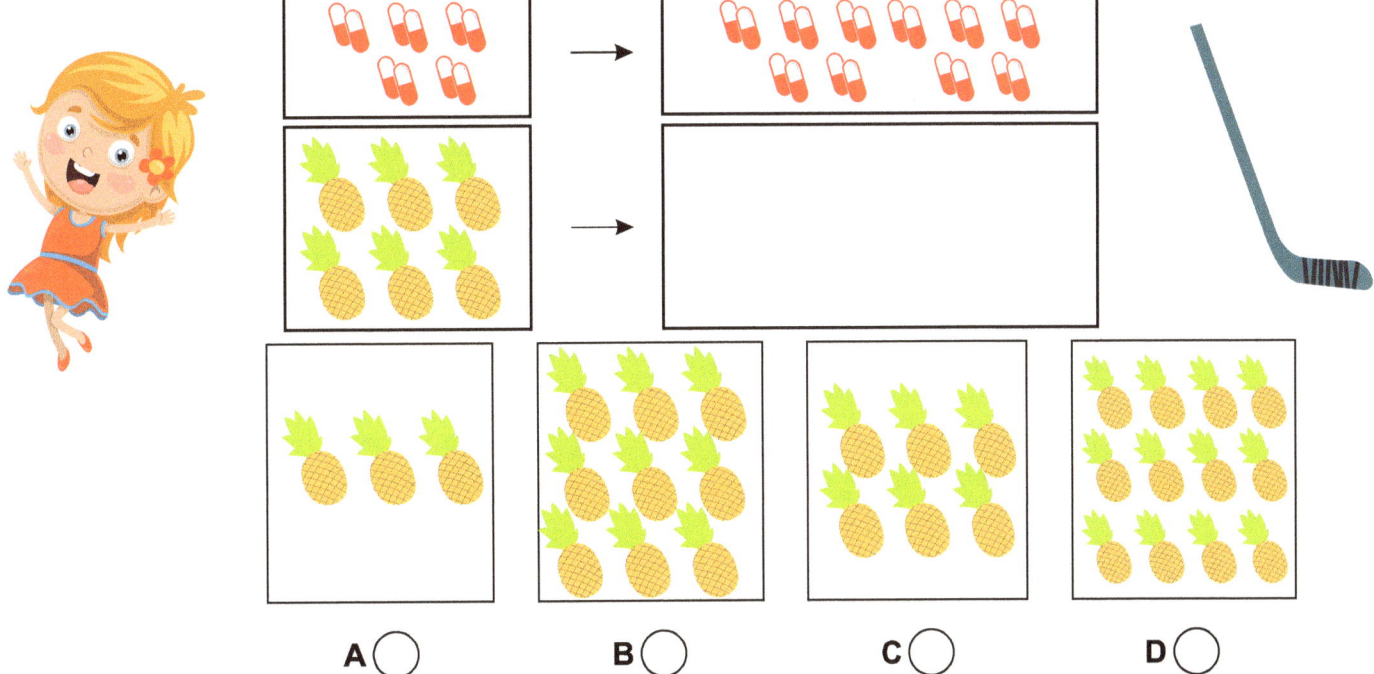

A ◯   B ◯   C ◯   D ◯

©All rights reserved-Math-Knots LLC., VA-USA
www.math-knots.com

Q-7

Look at the question with the Tennis Ball. Two boxes in the first row are related in a certain way which is similar to two boxes in the second row. Ava is trying to fill the bubble under the correct option. Help her to select from options A, B, C, and D.

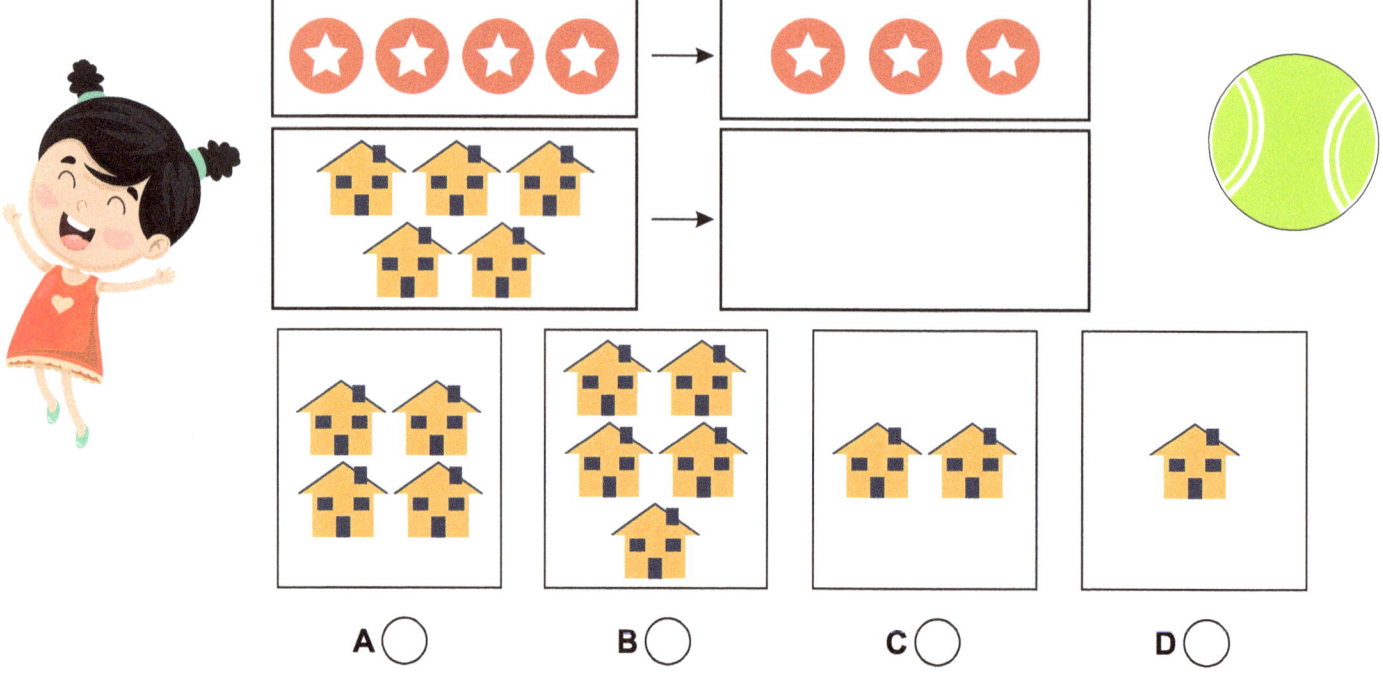

A ◯   B ◯   C ◯   D ◯

Q-8

Look at the question with the Cricket Bat. Two boxes in the first row are related in a certain way which is similar to two boxes in the second row. Johnson is trying to fill the bubble under the correct option. Help him to select from options A, B, C, and D.

A ◯   B ◯   C ◯   D ◯

©All rights reserved-Math-Knots LLC., VA-USA

www.math-knots.com

Q-9

Look at the question with the Boat. Two boxes in the first row are related in a certain way which is similar to two boxes in the second row. Alexander is trying to fill the bubble under the correct option. Help him to select from options A, B, C, and D.

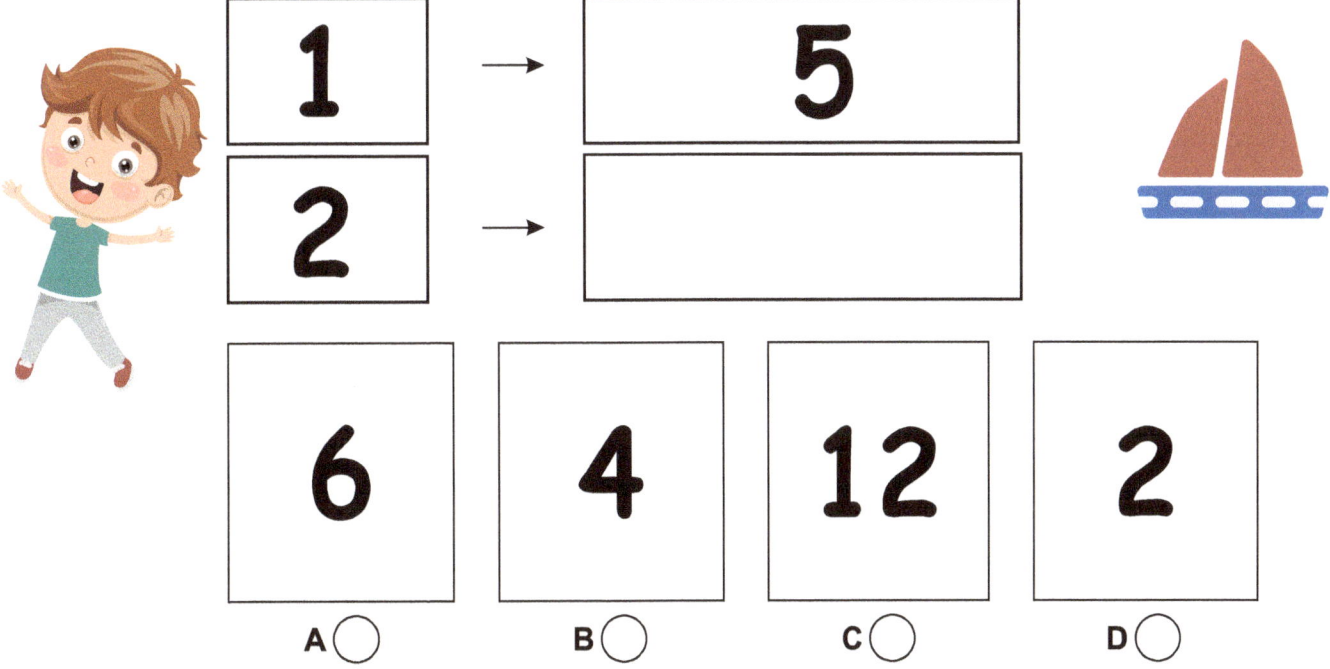

Q-10

Look at the question with the Ping-Pong bat. Two boxes in the first row are related in a certain way which is similar to two boxes in the second row. Lucas is trying to fill the bubble under the correct option. Help him to select from options A, B, C, and D.

Q-11 Look at the question with the Bicycle. Two boxes in the first row are related in a certain way which is similar to two boxes in the second row. Ella is trying to fill the bubble under the correct option. Help her to select from options A, B,C, and D.

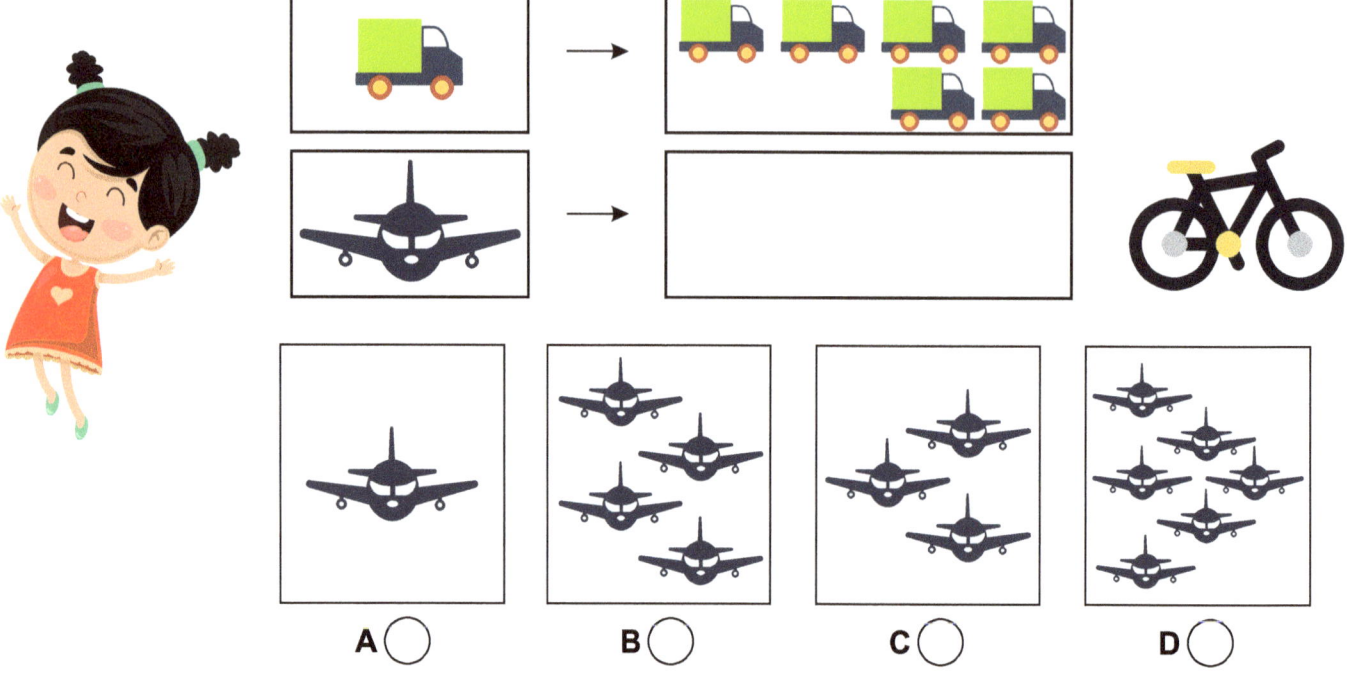

Q-12 Look at the question with the Dart Board. Two boxes in the first row are related in a certain way which is similar to two boxes in the second row. Samuel is trying to fill the bubble under the correct option. Help him to select from options A, B,C, and D.

Q-13

Look at the question with the Weights. Two boxes in the first row are related in a certain way which is similar to two boxes in the second row. Anthony is trying to fill the bubble under the correct option. Help him to select from options A, B, C, and D.

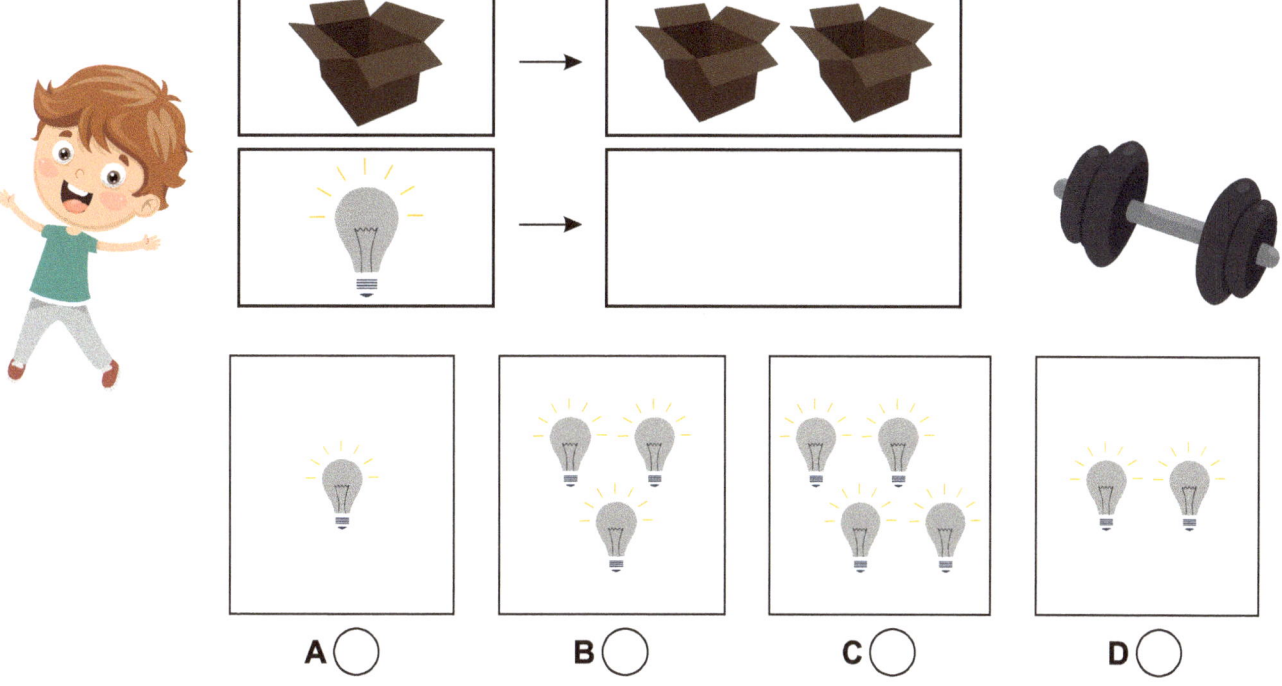

A ◯   B ◯   C ◯   D ◯

Q-14

Look at the question with the Skateboard. Two boxes in the first row are related in a certain way which is similar to two boxes in the second row. Skylar is trying to fill the bubble under the correct option. Help her to select from options A, B, C, and D.

A ◯   B ◯   C ◯   D ◯

©All rights reserved-Math-Knots LLC., VA-USA

www.math-knots.com

Q-15 Look at the question with the Karate Dress. Two boxes in the first row are related in a certain way which is similar to two boxes in the second row. Hannah is trying to fill the bubble under the correct option. Help her to select from options A, B, C, and D.

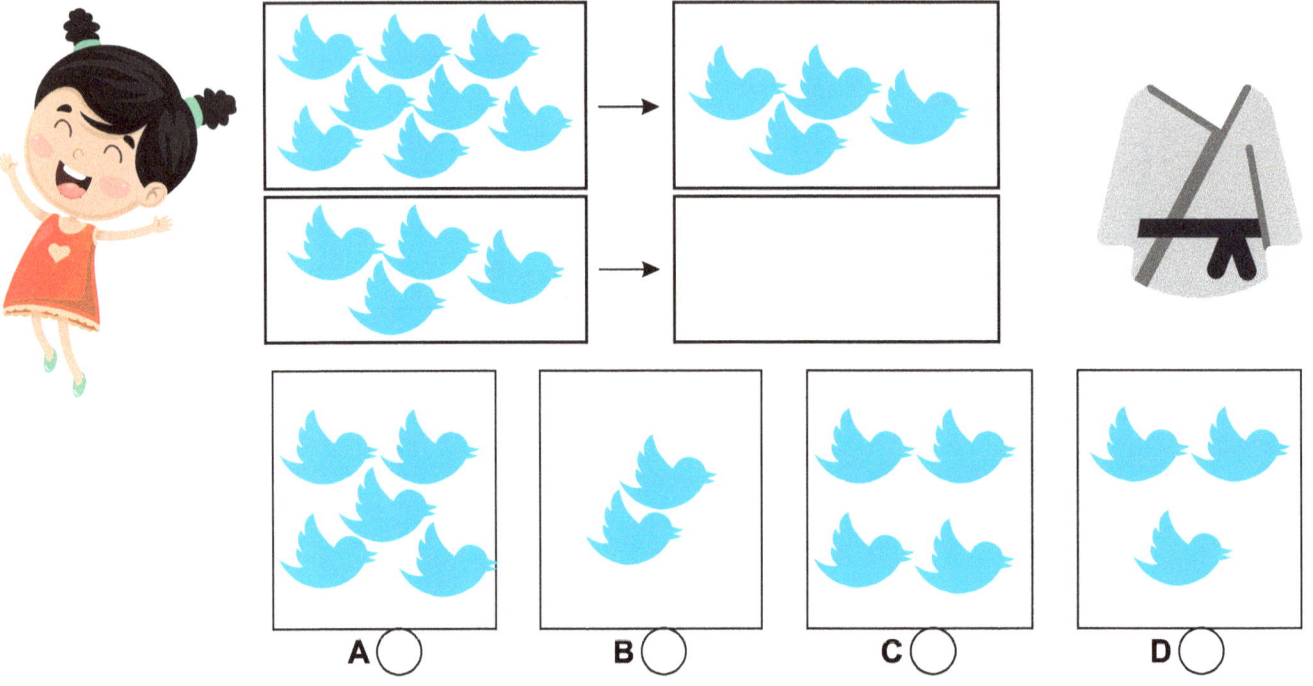

Q-16 Look at the question with the Swords. Two boxes in the first row are related in a certain way which is similar to two boxes in the second row. Mathew is trying to fill the bubble under the correct option. Help him to select from options A, B,C, and D.

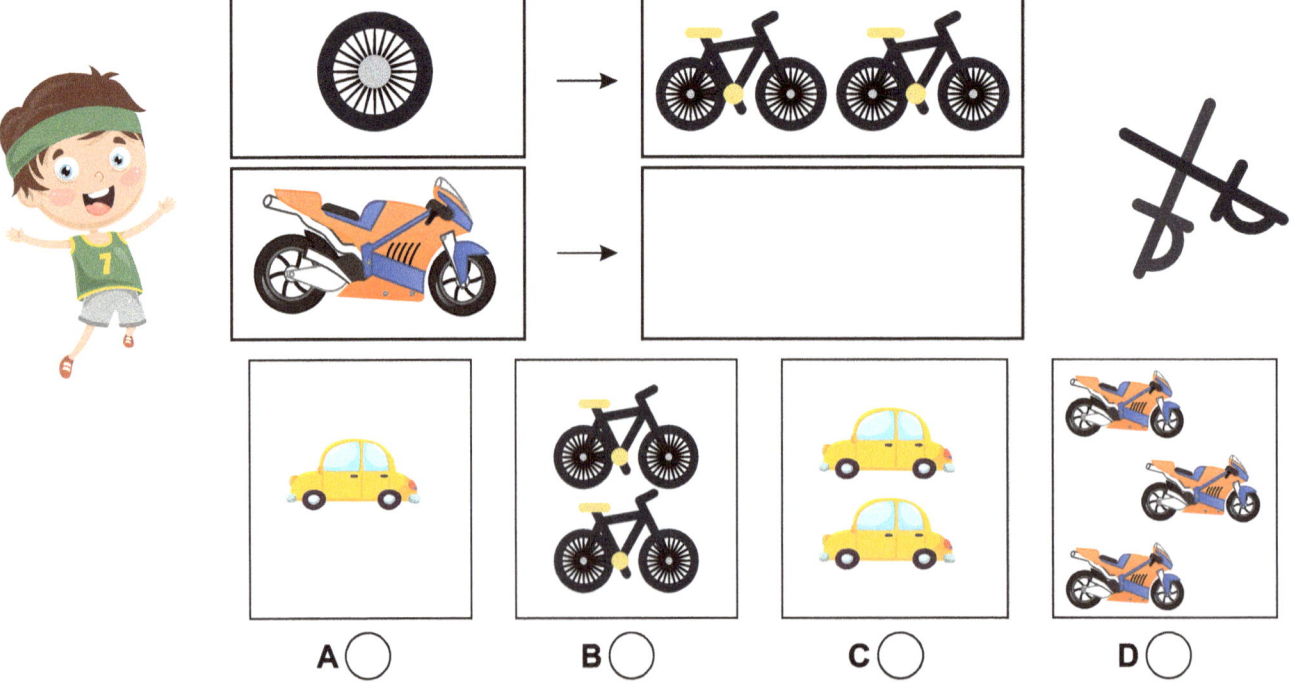

©All rights reserved-Math-Knots LLC., VA-USA

www.math-knots.com

Q-17

Look at the question with the Boxing Gloves. Two boxes in the first row are related in a certain way which is similar to two boxes in the second row. Joseph is trying to fill the bubble under the correct option. Help him to select from options A, B,C, and D.

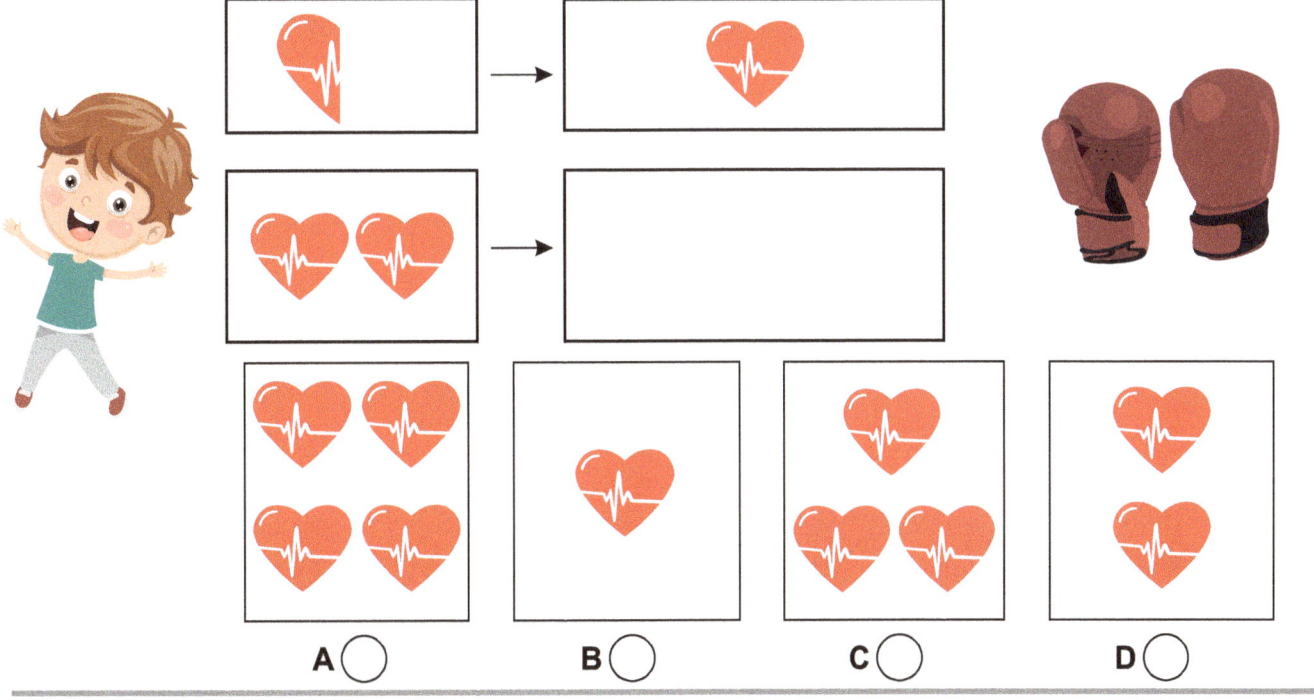

A ◯   **B** ◯   **C** ◯   **D** ◯

Q-18

Look at the question with the Racket. Two boxes in the first row are related in a certain way which is similar to two boxes in the second row. Chloe is trying to fill the bubble under the correct option. Help her to select from options A, B,C, and D.

A ◯   **B** ◯   **C** ◯   **D** ◯

©All rights reserved-Math-Knots LLC., VA-USA

TEST - 1

QUANTITATIVE APTITUDE

NUMBER SERIES

Lets Start the Test...

©All rights reserved-Math-Knots LLC., VA-USA

Sample

Look at the question with the Triangle. Cathy is making a pattern with her hexagon shaped beads. Can you help her to identify what goes in the empty string from the given four options A,B,C, and D.

A ◯   B ◯   C ◯   D ◯

Solution : C

3,4,5.....

The beads are increasing by 1. So next string should have six beads. Option C is the correct choice. The patterns can increase or decrease by a certain number of beads. Students are supposed to identify the correct pattern and answer the correct choice.

©All rights reserved-Math-Knots LLC., VA-USA
www.math-knots.com

©All rights reserved-Math-Knots LLC., VA-USA

Q-1 Look at the question with the Soccer Ball. Sam is making a pattern with his hexagon shaped beads. Can you help him to identify what goes in the empty string from the given four options A,B,C, and D.

A ◯   B ◯   C ◯   D ◯

Q-2 Look at the question with the Foot Ball. Mary is making a pattern with her hexagon shaped beads. Can you help her to identify what goes in the empty string from the given four options A,B,C, and D.

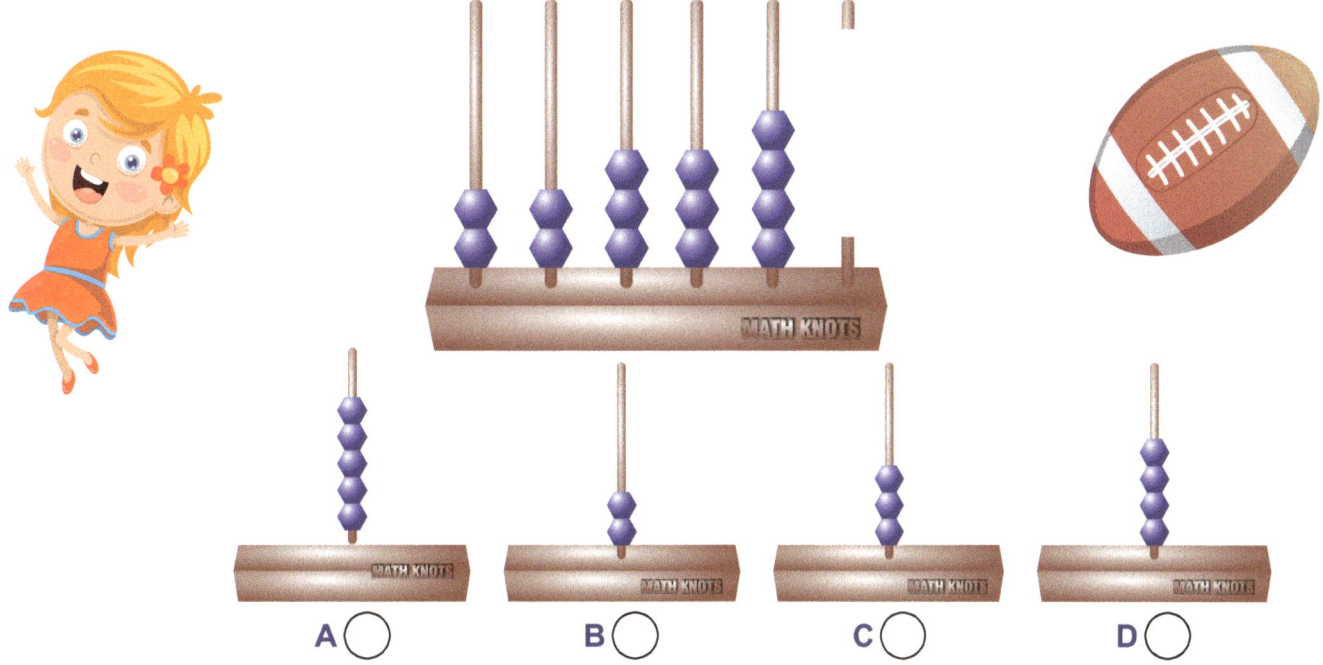

A ◯   B ◯   C ◯   D ◯

©All rights reserved-Math-Knots LLC., VA-USA

www.math-knots.com

QUANTITATIVE APTITUDE SECTION
NUMBER SERIES

Q-3

Look at the question with the Basket Ball. Maria is making a pattern with her hexagon shaped beads. Can you help her to identify what goes in the empty string from the given four options A, B, C, and D.

A ◯ B ◯ C ◯ D ◯

Q-4

Look at the question with the Shuttlecock. Dan is making a pattern with his hexagon shaped beads. Can you help him to identify what goes in the empty string from the given four options A, B, C, and D.

A ◯ B ◯ C ◯ D ◯

©All rights reserved-Math-Knots LLC., VA-USA

www.math-knots.com

Q-5

Look at the question with the Bowling Pin. Robert is making a pattern with his hexagon shaped beads. Can you help him to identify what goes in the empty string from the given four options A, B, C, and D.

A ⃝   B ⃝   C ⃝   D ⃝

Q-6

Look at the question with the Hockey Stick. Kate is making a pattern with her hexagon shaped beads. Can you help her to identify what goes in the empty string from the given four options A, B, C, and D.

A ⃝   B ⃝   C ⃝   D ⃝

Q-7

Look at the question with the Tennis Ball. Jane is making a pattern with her hexagon shaped beads. Can you help her to identify what goes in the empty string from the given four options A,B,C, and D.

A ○   B ○   C ○   D ○

Q-8

Look at the question with the Cricket Bat. Johnson is making a pattern with his hexagon shaped beads. Can you help him to identify what goes in the empty string from the given four options A,B,C, and D.

A ○   B ○   C ○   D ○

©All rights reserved-Math-Knots LLC., VA-USA

www.math-knots.com

Q-9

Look at the question with the Boat. Smitha, is making a pattern with her hexagon shaped beads. Can you help her to identify what goes in the empty string from the given four options A,B,C, and D.

A ◯   B ◯   C ◯   D ◯

Q-10

Look at the question with the Baseball Bat. Adam is making a pattern with his hexagon shaped beads. Can you help him to identify what goes in the empty string from the given four options A,B,C, and D.

A ◯   B ◯   C ◯   D ◯

©All rights reserved-Math-Knots LLC., VA-USA

www.math-knots.com

Q-11

Look at the question with the Bicycle. Alvin is making a pattern with her hexagon shaped beads. Can you help her to identify what goes in the empty string from the given four options A, B, C, and D.

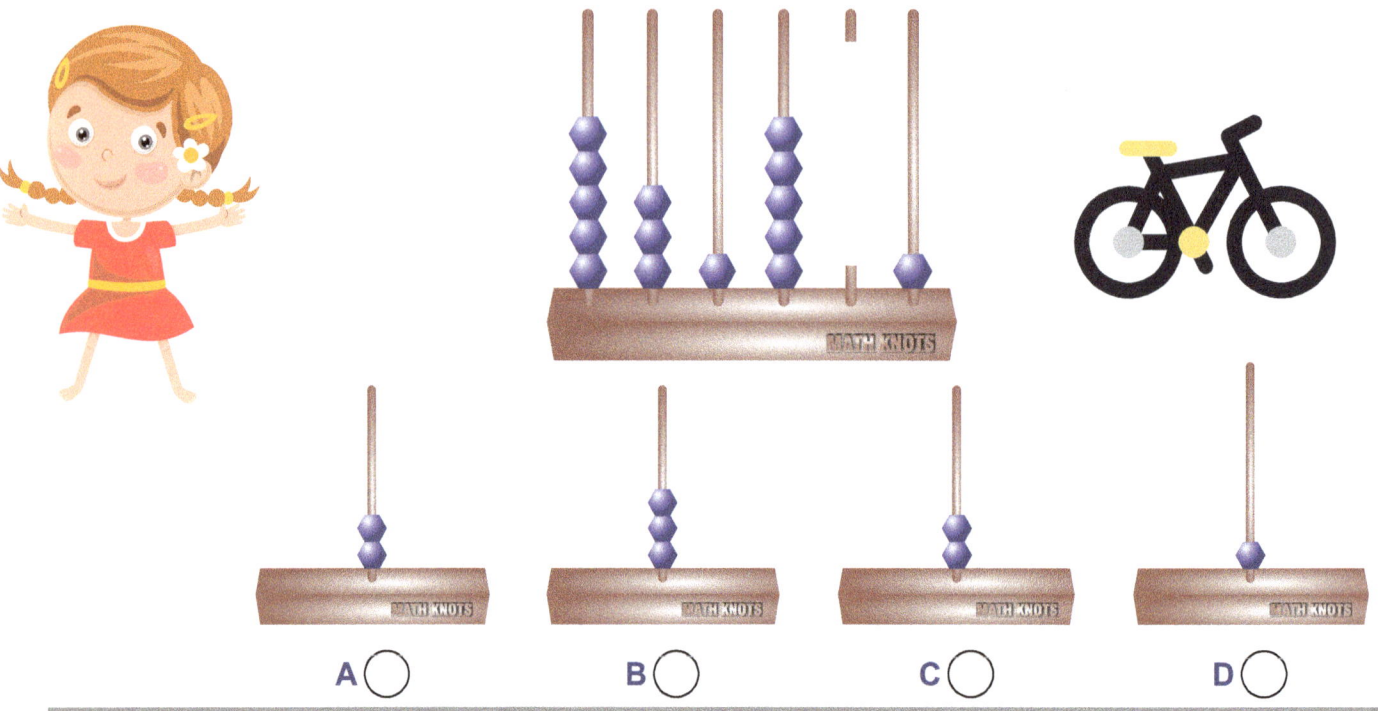

A ◯   B ◯   C ◯   D ◯

Q-12

Look at the question with the Dart Board. John is making a pattern with his hexagon shaped beads. Can you help him to identify what goes in the empty string from the given four options A, B, C, and D.

A ◯   B ◯   C ◯   D ◯

©All rights reserved-Math-Knots LLC., VA-USA

www.math-knots.com

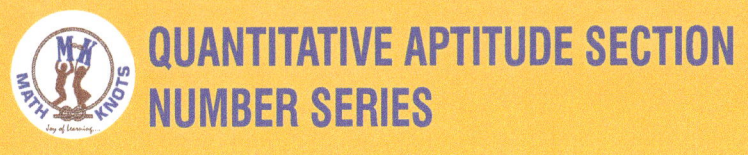

Q-13 Look at the question with the Weights. Lisa is making a pattern with her hexagon shaped beads. Can you help her to identify what goes in the empty string from the given four options A,B,C, and D.

A ◯   B ◯   C ◯   D ◯

Q-14 Look at the question with the Ping-Pong Bats. Emma is making a pattern with her hexagon shaped beads. Can you help her to identify what goes in the empty string from the given four options A B,C,and D.

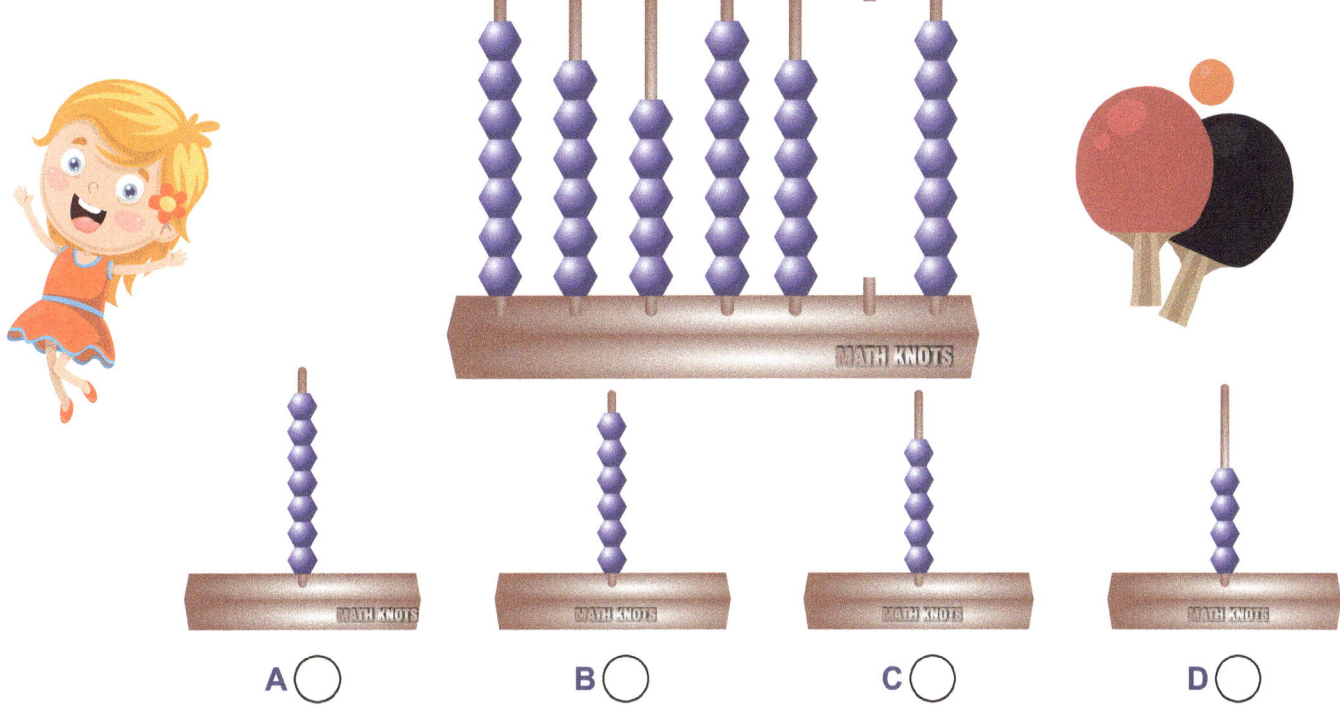

A ◯   B ◯   C ◯   D ◯

©All rights reserved-Math-Knots LLC., VA-USA

71

Q-15 Look at the question with the Karate Dress. Kathy is making a pattern with her hexagon shaped beads. Can you help her to identify what goes in the empty string from the given four options A,B,C, and D.

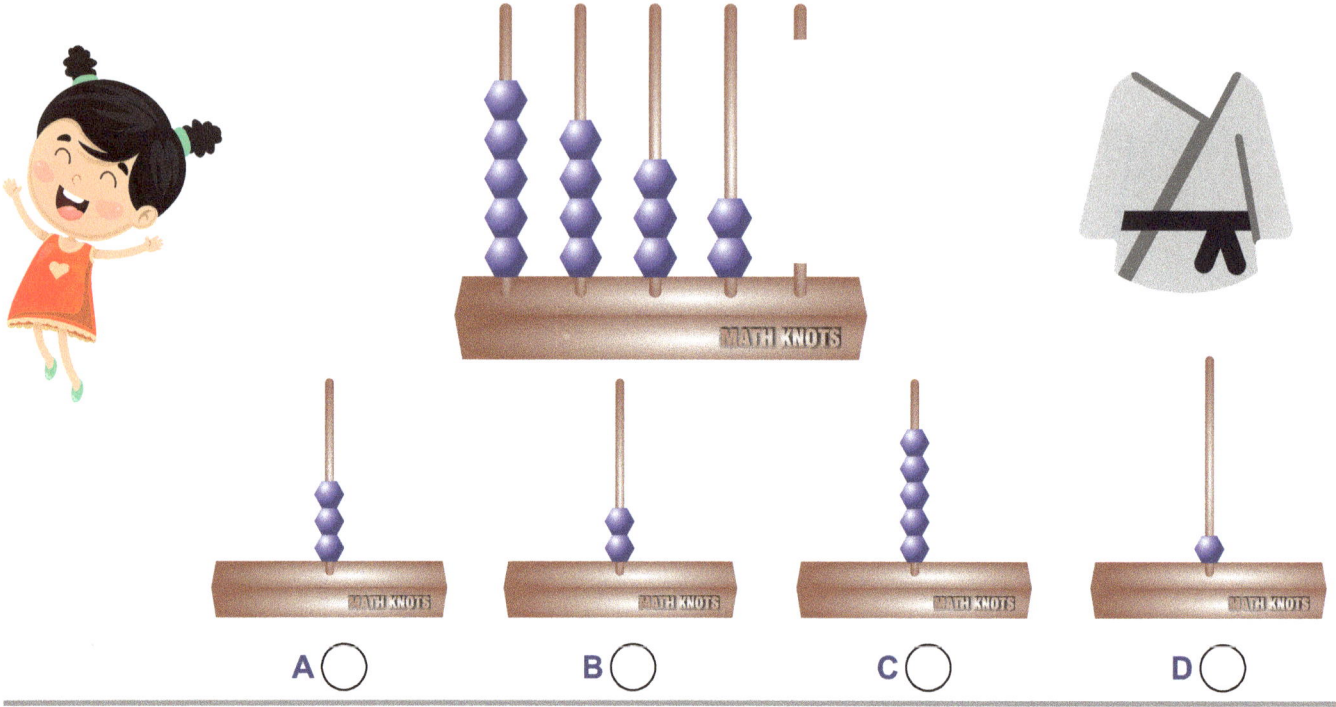

A ◯   B ◯   C ◯   D ◯

Q-16 Look at the question with the Swords. Berry is making a pattern with his hexagon shaped beads. Can you help him to identify what goes in the empty string from the given four options A,B,C, and D.

A ◯   B ◯   C ◯   D ◯

©All rights reserved-Math-Knots LLC., VA-USA

www.math-knots.com

Q-17 Look at the question with the Boxing Gloves. Charles is making a pattern with his hexagon shaped beads. Can you help him to identify what goes in the empty string from the given four options A, B, C, and D.

A ◯   B ◯   C ◯   D ◯

Q-18 Look at the question with the Racket. Claud is making a pattern with her hexagon shaped beads. Can you help her to identify what goes in the empty string from the given four options A, B, C, and D.

A ◯   B ◯   C ◯   D ◯

©All rights reserved-Math-Knots LLC., VA-USA
www.math-knots.com

©All rights reserved-Math-Knots LLC., VA-USA

TEST - 1

QUANTITATIVE APTITUDE

NUMBER PUZZLES

Lets Start the Test...

©All rights reserved-Math-Knots LLC., VA-USA

www.math-knots.com

©All rights reserved-Math-Knots LLC., VA-USA

Sample Look at the question and put your finger on the Guitar. Ryan is wondering what is the missing number under the question mark ? Help him to find the missing number under the question mark and fill in the bubble.

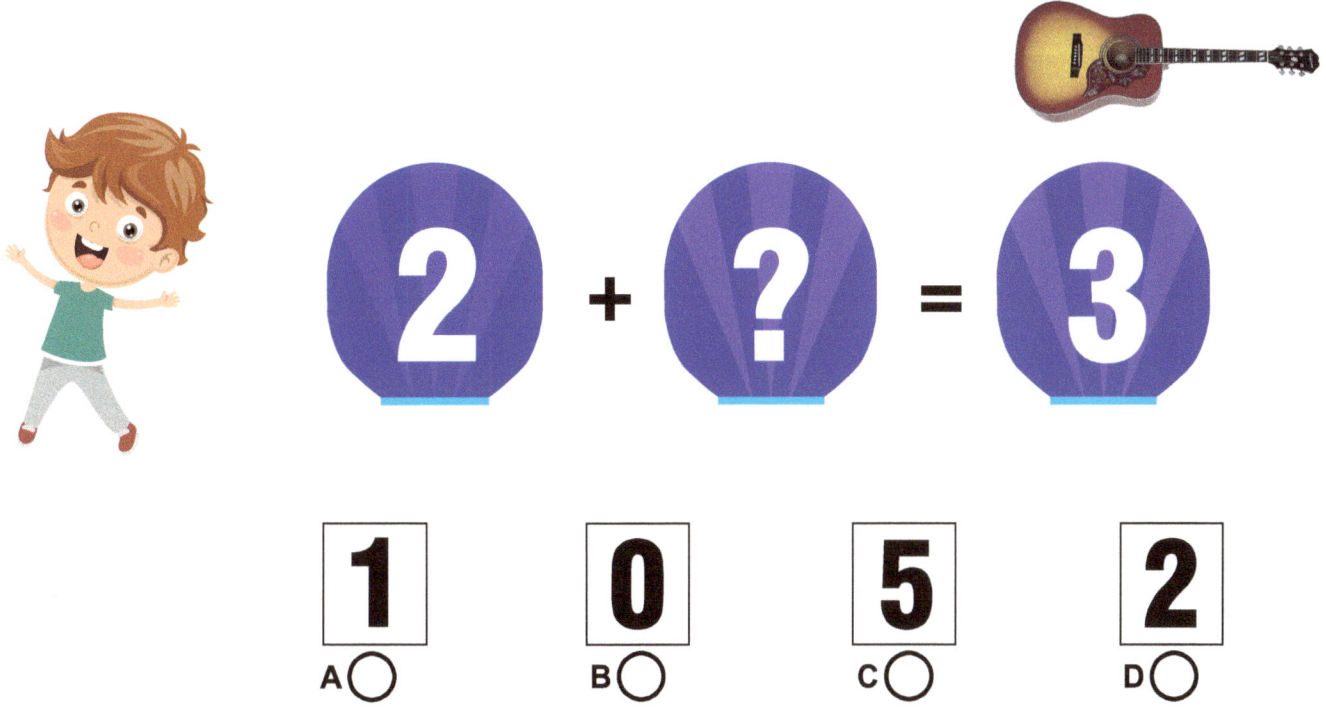

2 + ? = 3

A ◯ 1   B ◯ 0   C ◯ 5   D ◯ 2

Solution : A

How much should be added to 2 to make it 3

3 - 2 = 1

Meaning if we add 1 to 2 we get a total of three

©All rights reserved-Math-Knots LLC., VA-USA

www.math-knots.com

©All rights reserved-Math-Knots LLC., VA-USA

www.math-knots.com

Q-1 Look at the question with Soccer Ball. Fred is wondering what is the missing number under the question mark ? Help him to find the missing number under the question mark and fill in the bubble.

5	**6**	**1**	**0**
A ○	B ○	C ○	D ○

Q-2 Look at the question with Foot Ball. Mary is wondering what is the missing number under the question mark ? Help her to find the missing number under the question mark and fill in the bubble.

5	**4**	**1**	**6**
A ○	B ○	C ○	D ○

©All rights reserved-Math-Knots LLC., VA-USA
www.math-knots.com

Q-3 Look at the question with Basket Ball. James is wondering what is the missing number under the question mark ? Help him to find the missing number under the question mark and fill in the bubble.

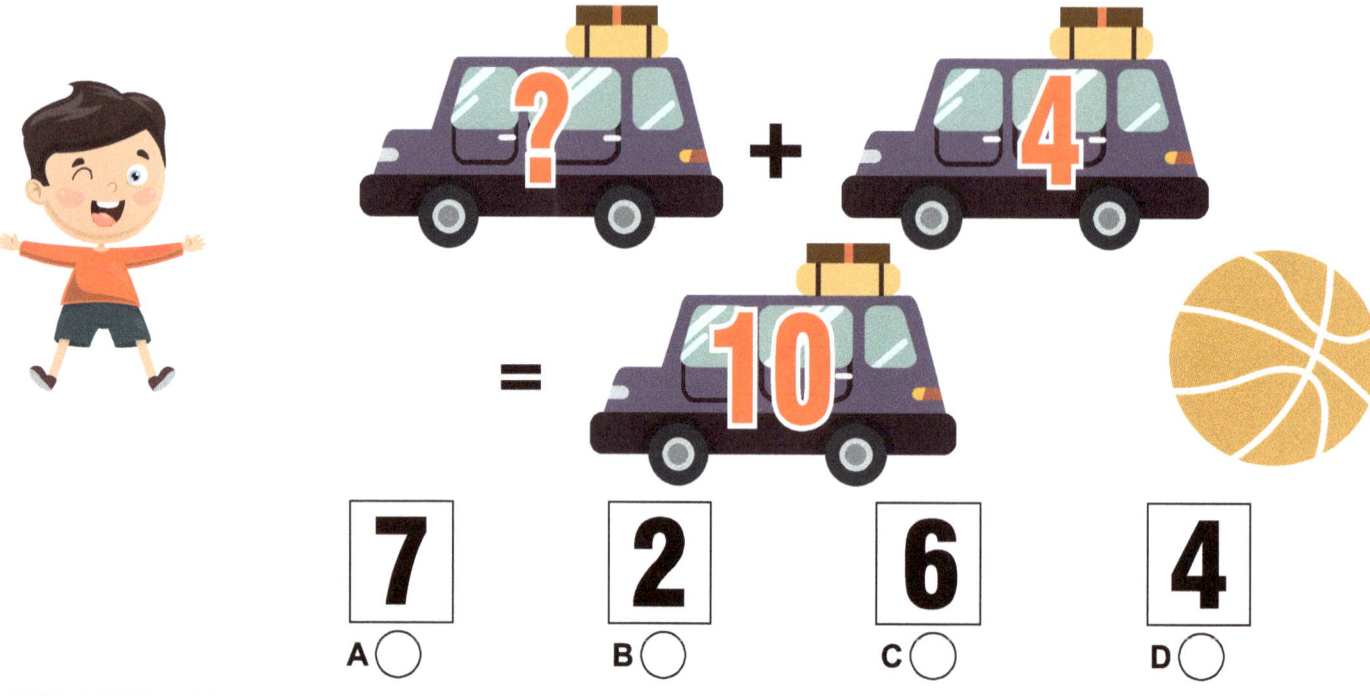

7	2	6	4
A○	B○	C○	D○

Q-4 Look at the question with Shuttlecock. Alfred is wondering what is the missing number under the question mark ? Help him to find the missing number under the question mark and fill in the bubble.

4	0	3	2
A○	B○	C○	D○

©All rights reserved-Math-Knots LLC., VA-USA

www.math-knots.com

Q-5 Look at the question with Bowling Pin. Jason is wondering what is the missing number under the question mark ? Help him to find the missing number under the question mark and fill in the bubble.

2	4	5	3
A ○	B ○	C ○	D ○

Q-6 Look at the question with Hockey Stick. Jia is wondering what is the missing number under the question mark ? Help her to find the missing number under the question mark and fill in the bubble.

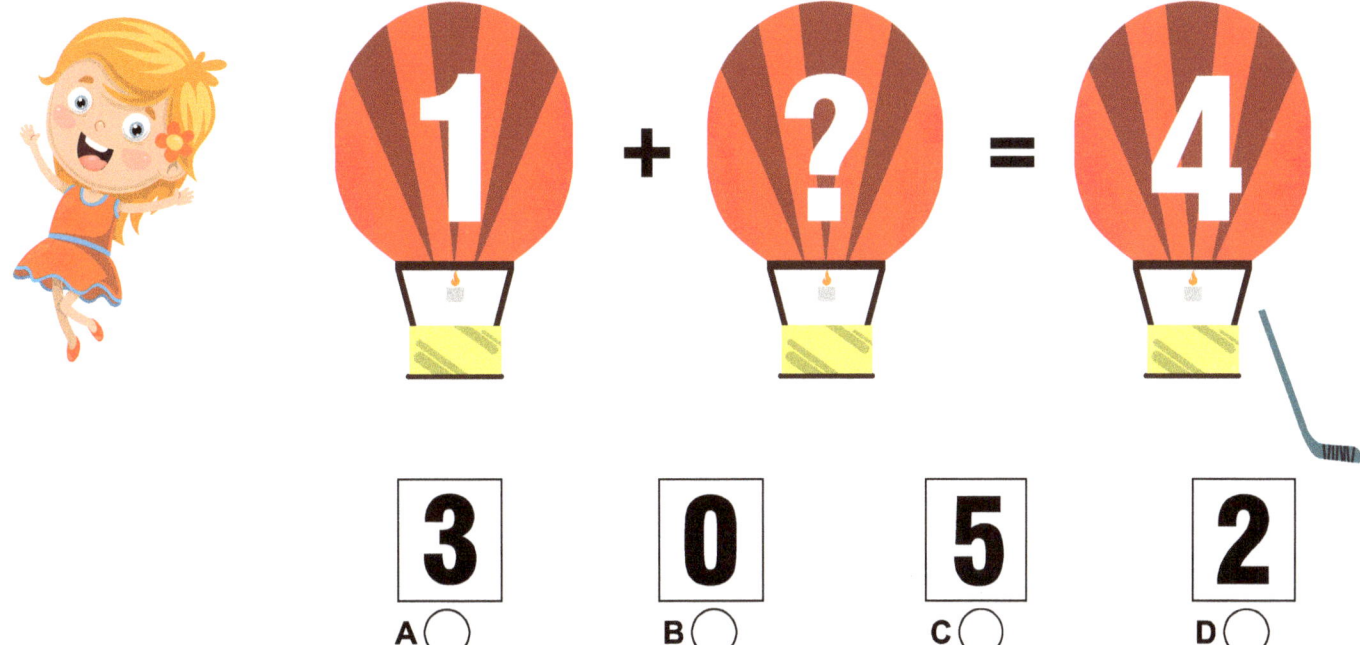

3	0	5	2
A ○	B ○	C ○	D ○

©All rights reserved-Math-Knots LLC., VA-USA
www.math-knots.com

Q-7 Look at the question with Tennis Ball. Olivia is wondering what is the missing number under the question mark? Help her to find the missing number under the question mark and fill in the bubble.

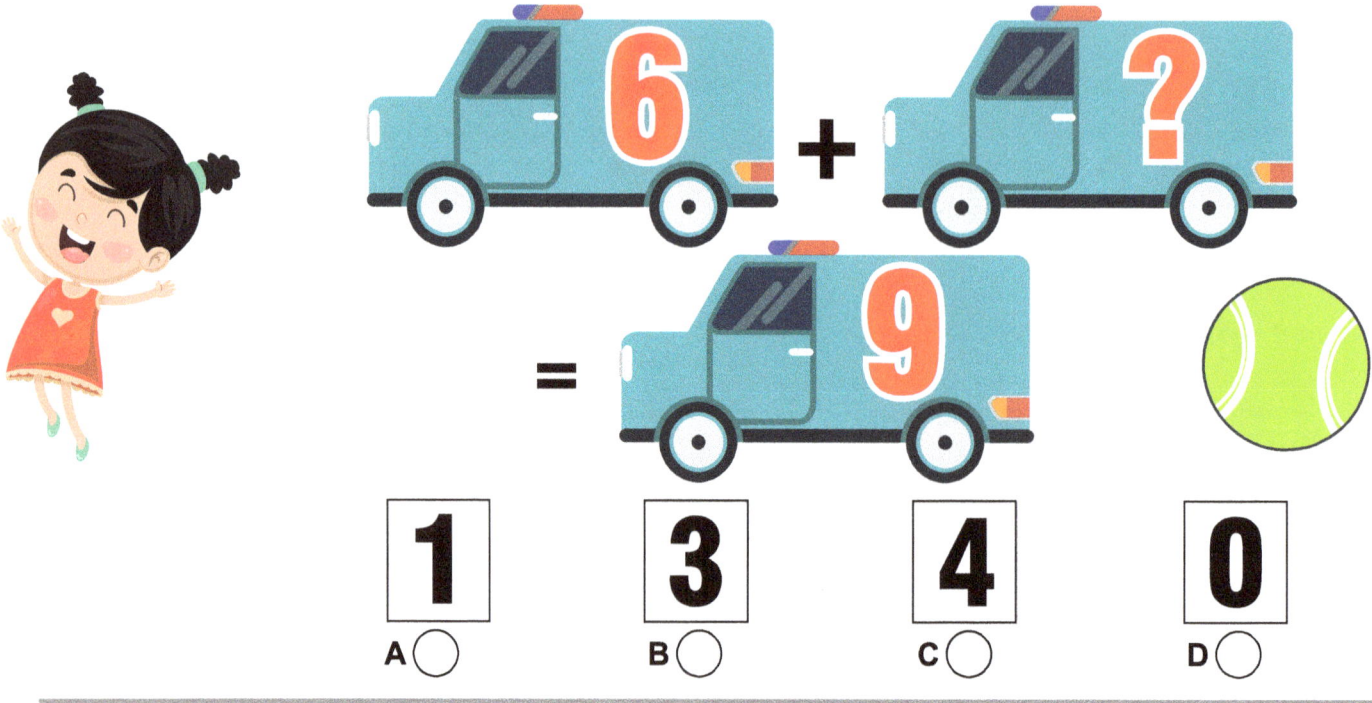

$$6 + ? = 9$$

1	3	4	0
A◯	B◯	C◯	D◯

Q-8 Look at the question with Cricket Bat. Michael is wondering what is the missing number under the question mark? Help him to find the missing number under the question mark and fill in the bubble.

$$4 + 6 + 4 = ?$$

10	11	12	14
A◯	B◯	C◯	D◯

©All rights reserved-Math-Knots LLC., VA-USA

www.math-knots.com

Q-9 Look at the question with Boat. Hope is wondering what is the missing number under the question mark ? Help her to find the missing number under the question mark and fill in the bubble.

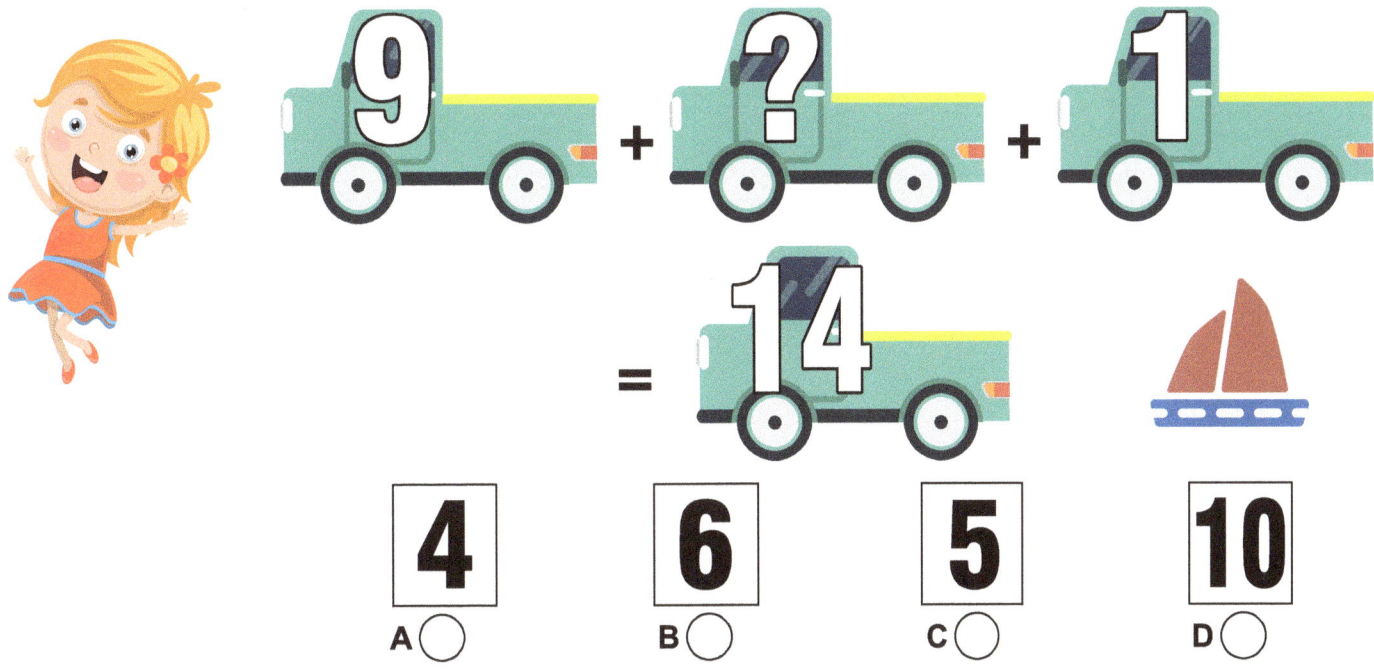

A◯ 4   B◯ 6   C◯ 5   D◯ 10

Q-10 Look at the question with Pin-Pong Bat. Ethen is wondering what is the missing number under the question mark ? Help him to find the missing number under the question mark and fill in the bubble.

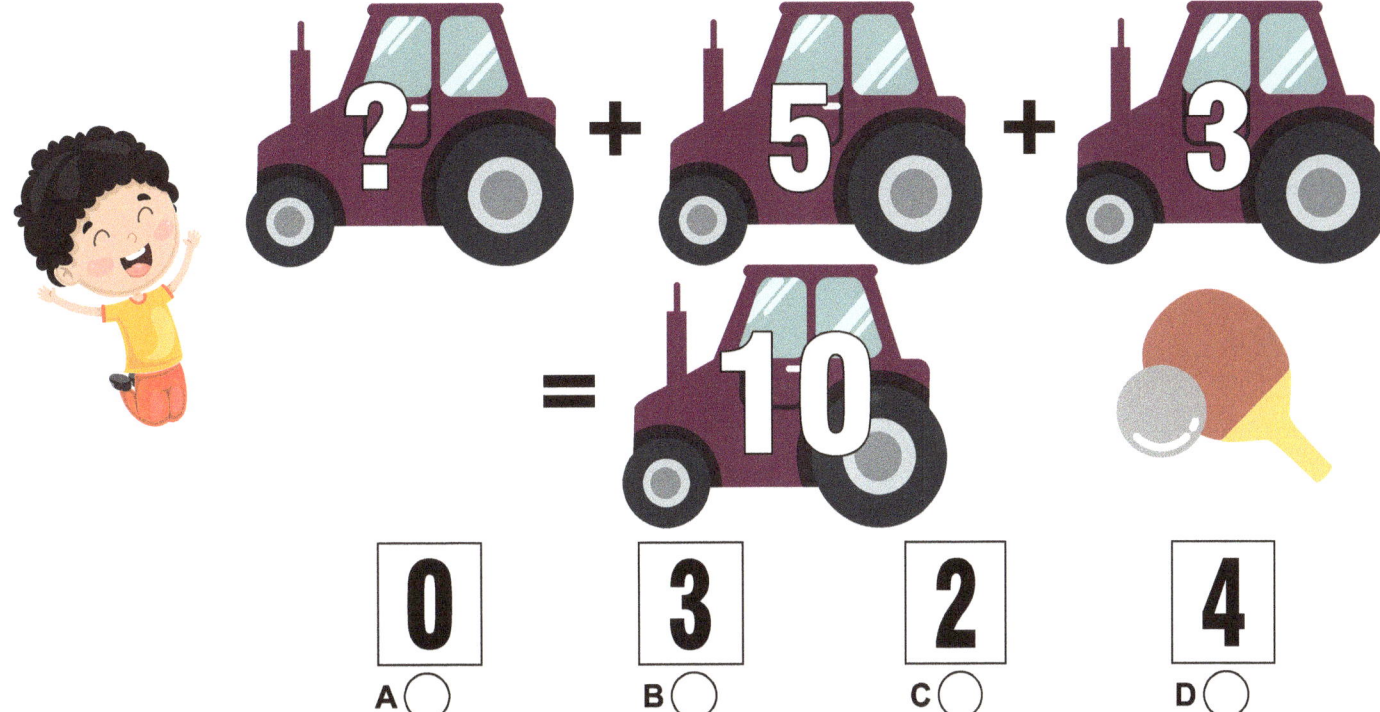

A◯ 0   B◯ 3   C◯ 2   D◯ 4

©All rights reserved-Math-Knots LLC., VA-USA

Q-11

Look at the question with Bicycle. Elizabeth is wondering what is the missing number under the question mark ? Help her to find the missing number under the question mark and fill in the bubble.

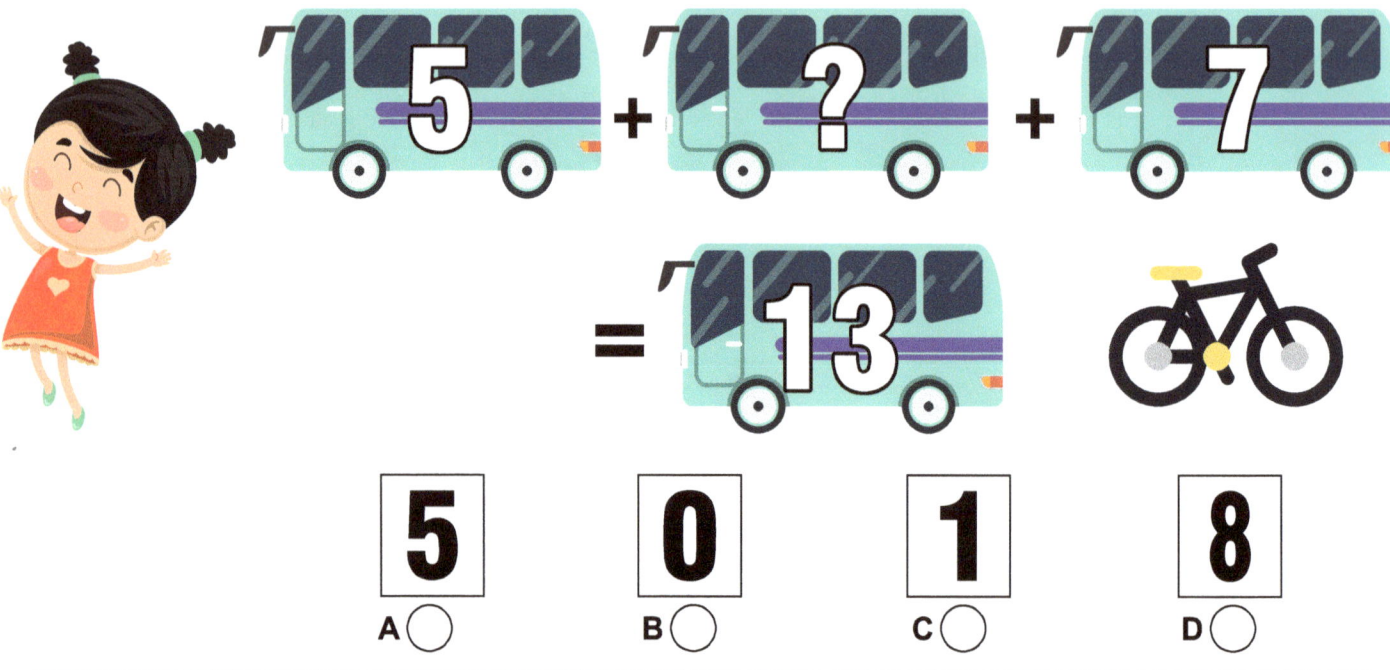

A. 5

B. 0

C. 1

D. 8

Q-12

Look at the question with Dart Board. Logan is wondering what is the missing number under the question mark ? Help him to find the missing number under the question mark and fill in the bubble.

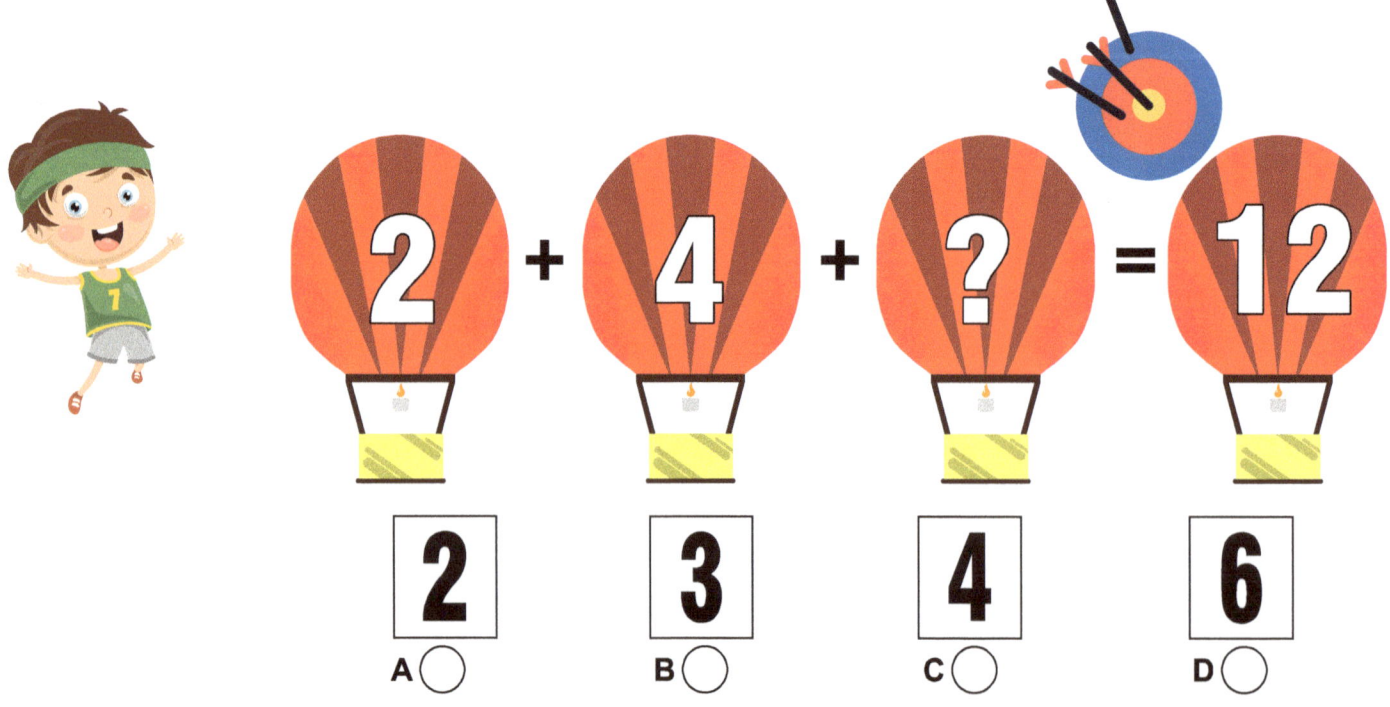

A. 2

B. 3

C. 4

D. 6

Q-13 Look at the question with Weights. Olivia is wondering what is the missing number under the question mark ? Help her to find the missing number under the question mark and fill in the bubble.

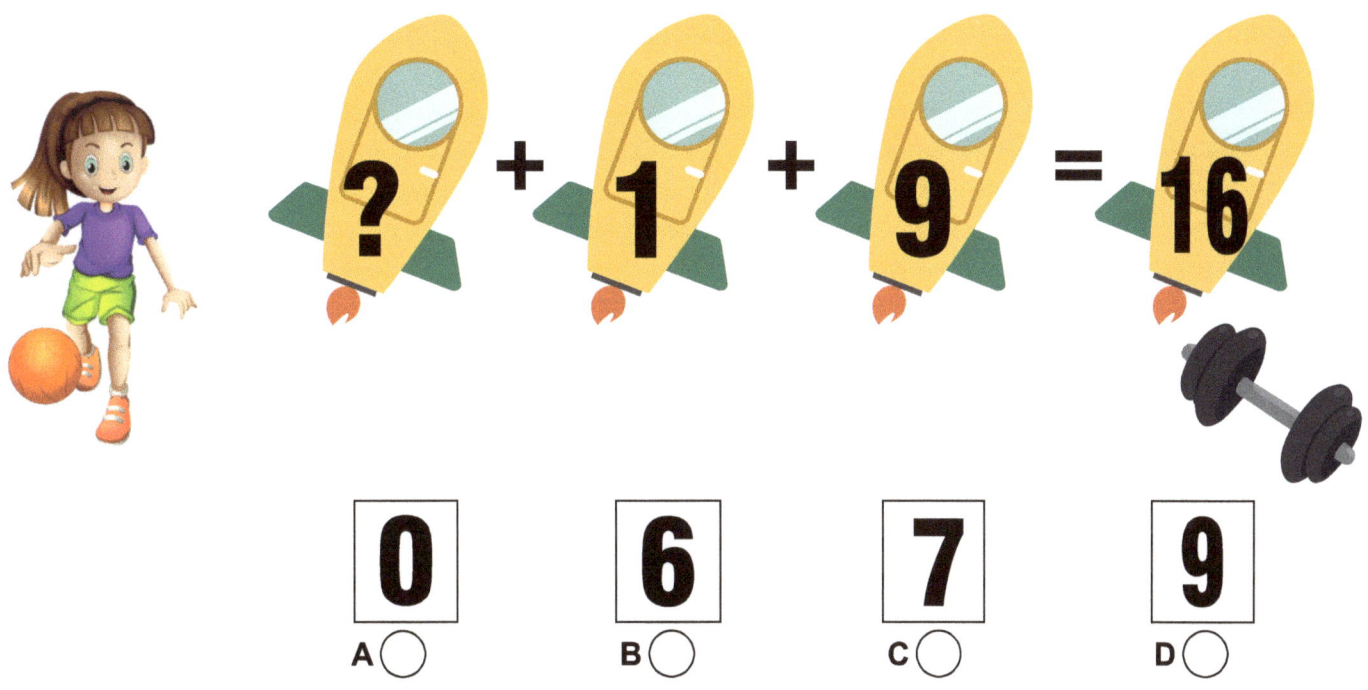

0	6	7	9
A○	B○	C○	D○

Q-14 Look at the question with Skate Board. Grace is wondering what is the missing number under the question mark ? Help her to find the missing number under the question mark and fill in the bubble.

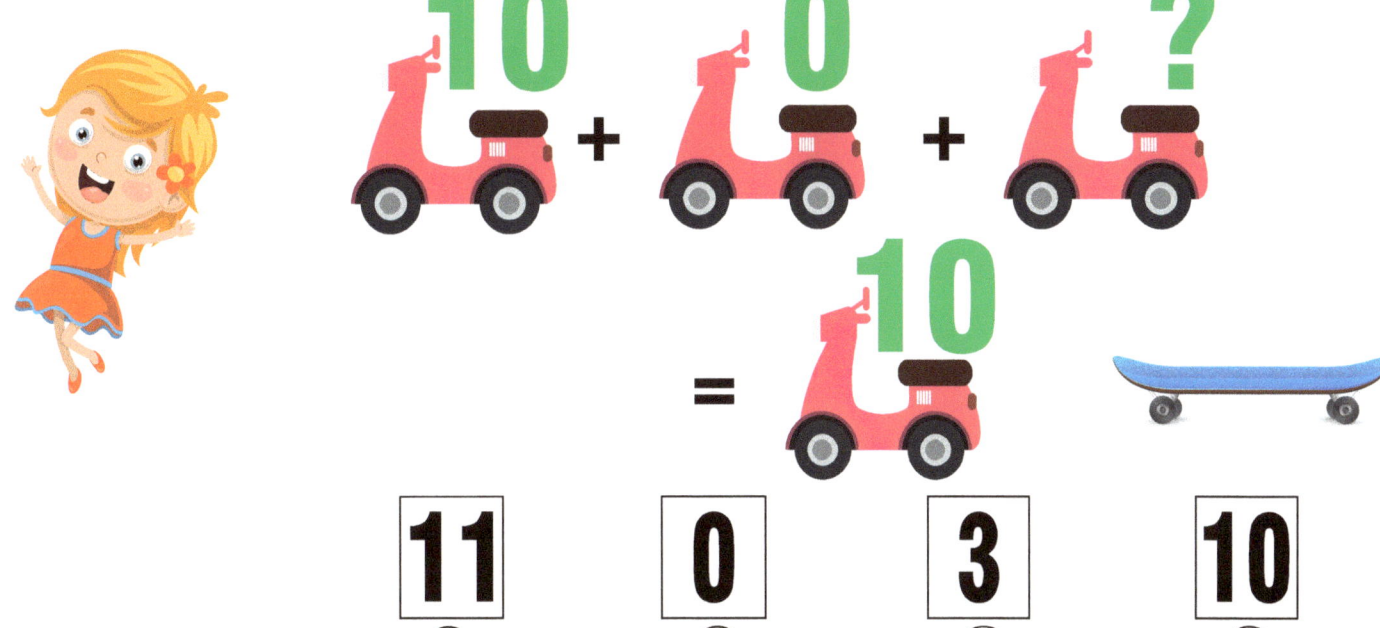

11	0	3	10
A○	B○	C○	D○

Q-15 Look at the question with Karate Dress. Sophia is wondering what is the missing number under the question mark ? Help her to find the missing number under the question mark and fill in the bubble.

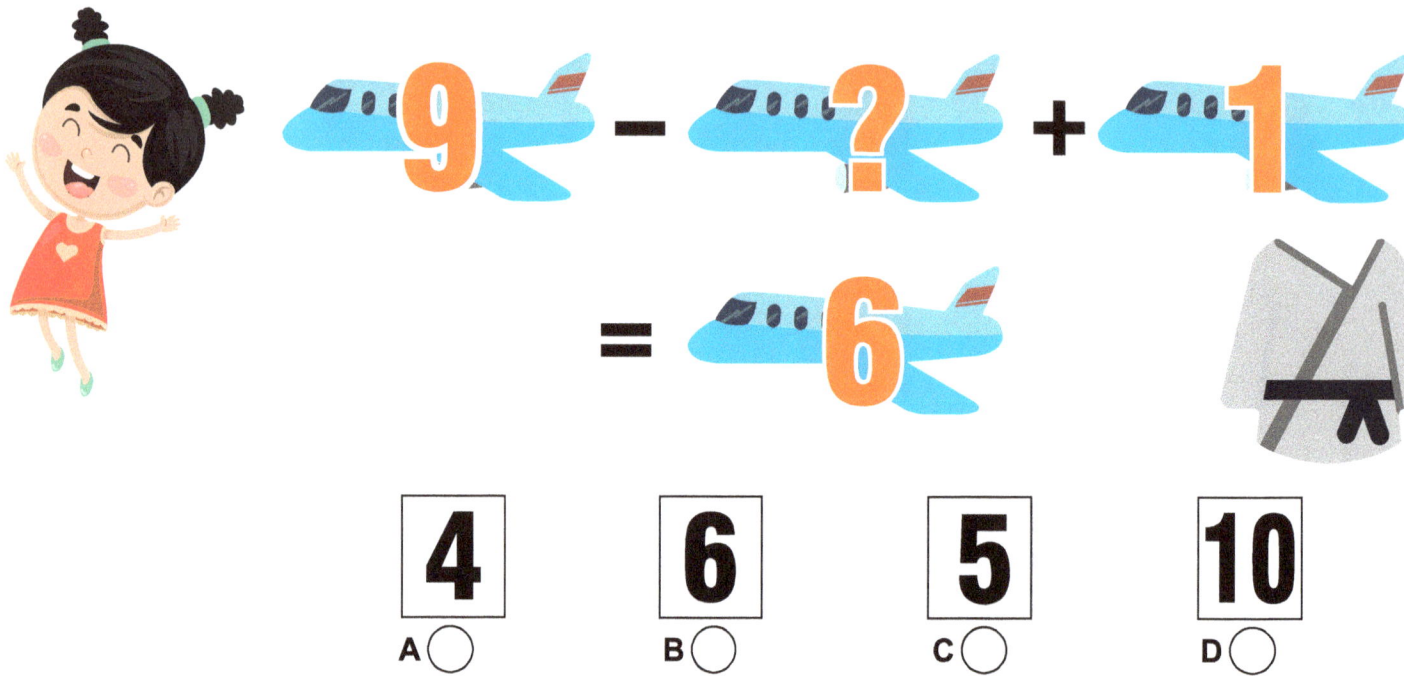

4	6	5	10
A ◯	B ◯	C ◯	D ◯

Q-16 Look at the question with Swords. Jackson is wondering what is the missing number under the question mark ? Help him to find the missing number under the question mark and fill in the bubble.

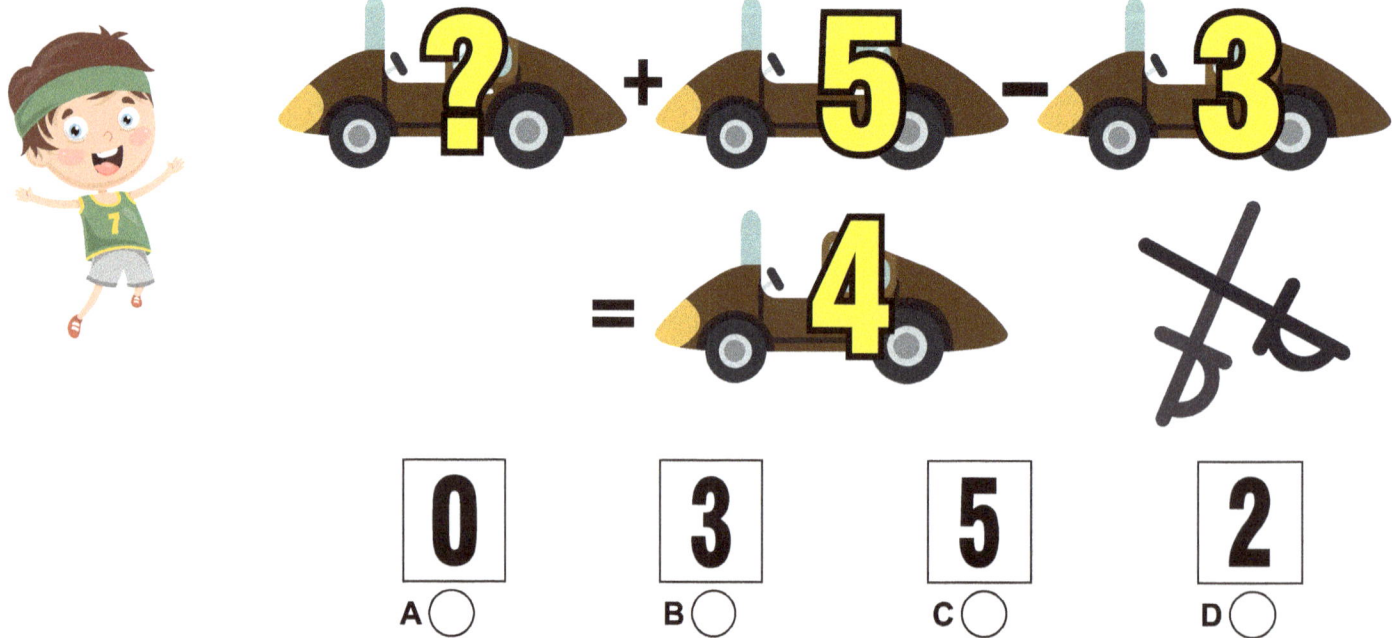

0	3	5	2
A ◯	B ◯	C ◯	D ◯

©All rights reserved-Math-Knots LLC., VA-USA
www.math-knots.com

Q-17

Look at the question with Boxing gloves. Mathew is wondering what is the missing number under the question mark ? Help him to find the missing number under the question mark and fill in the bubble.

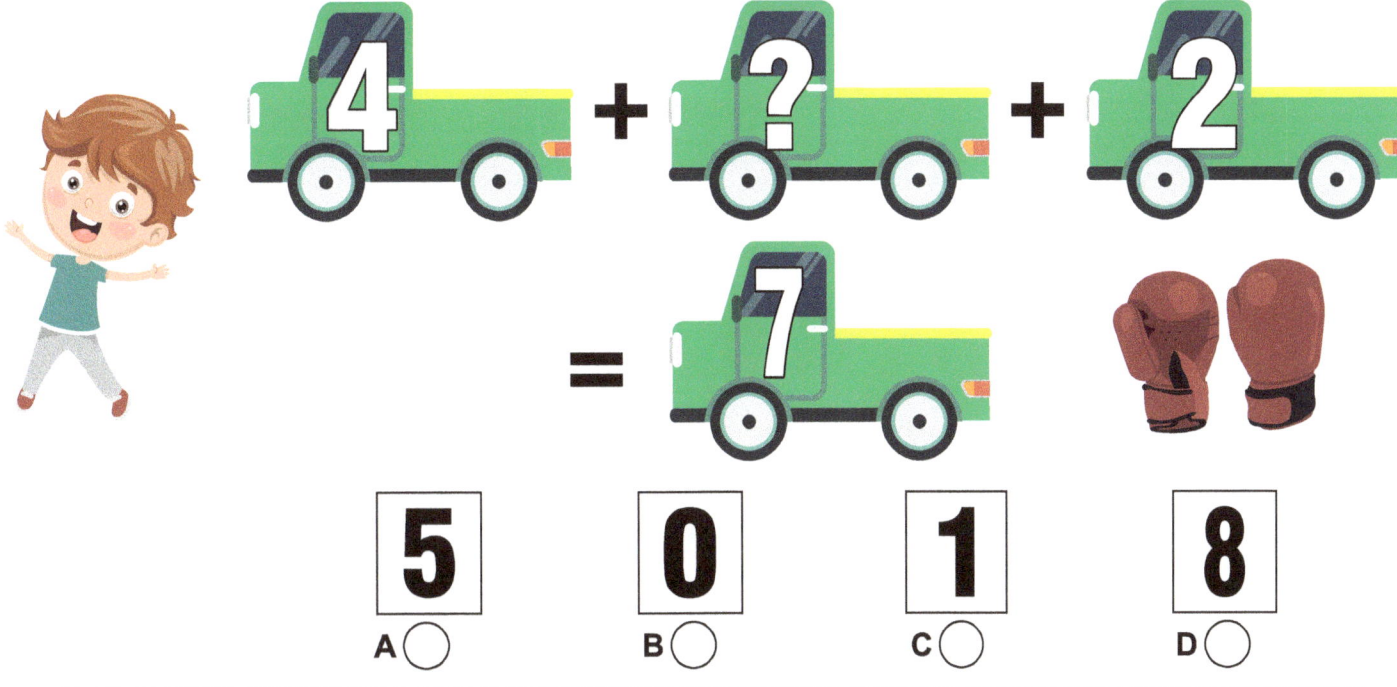

A	B	C	D
5 ◯	0 ◯	1 ◯	8 ◯

Q-18

Look at the question with Racket. Sofia is wondering what is the missing number under the question mark ? Help her to find the missing number under the question mark and fill in the bubble.

A	B	C	D
2 ◯	11 ◯	1 ◯	0 ◯

©All rights reserved-Math-Knots LLC., VA-USA
www.math-knots.com

Q-19 Look at the question with Skate Board. Benjamin is wondering what is the missing number under the question mark ? Help him to find the missing number under the question mark and fill in the bubble.

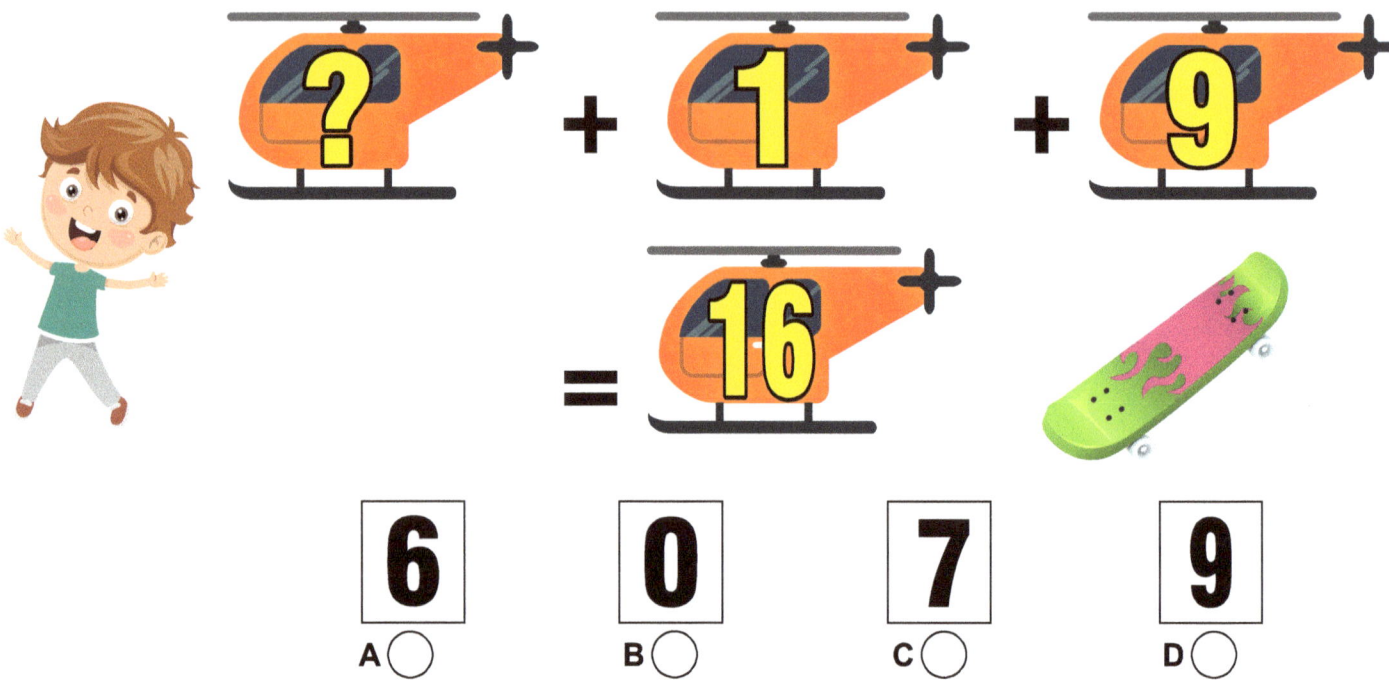

A ○ 6 B ○ 0 C ○ 7 D ○ 9

Q-20 Look at the question with Baseball Bat. Carol is wondering what is the missing number under the question mark ? Help her to find the missing number under the question mark and fill in the bubble.

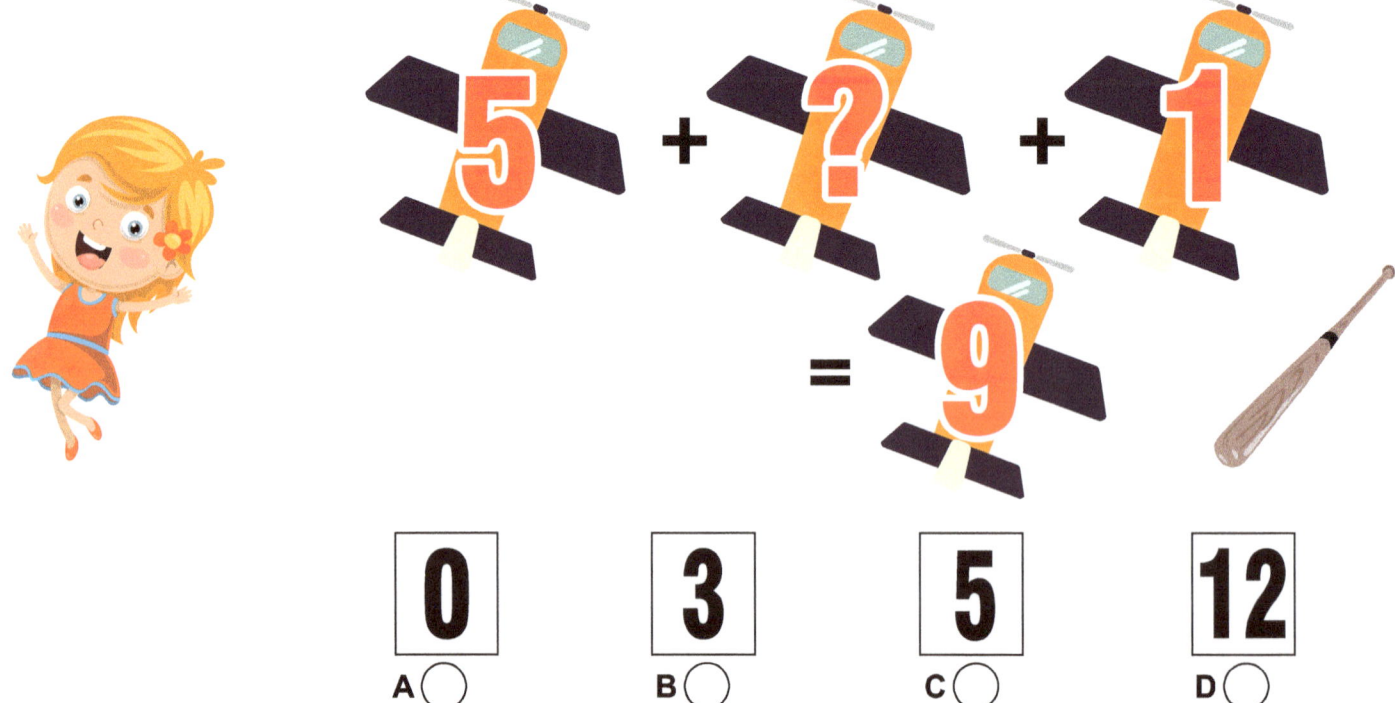

A ○ 0 B ○ 3 C ○ 5 D ○ 12

©All rights reserved-Math-Knots LLC., VA-USA
www.math-knots.com

TEST - 1

NON VERBAL SECTION

FIGURE MATRICES

Lets Start the Test...

©All rights reserved-Math-Knots LLC., VA-USA

www.math-knots.com

©All rights reserved-Math-Knots LLC., VA-USA

Sample Look at the question with the Tree. The first three pictures belong to one group in a common way. Help Bob to find out which of the below options belong to the same group. Identify the correct picture and help him to bubble the right choice.

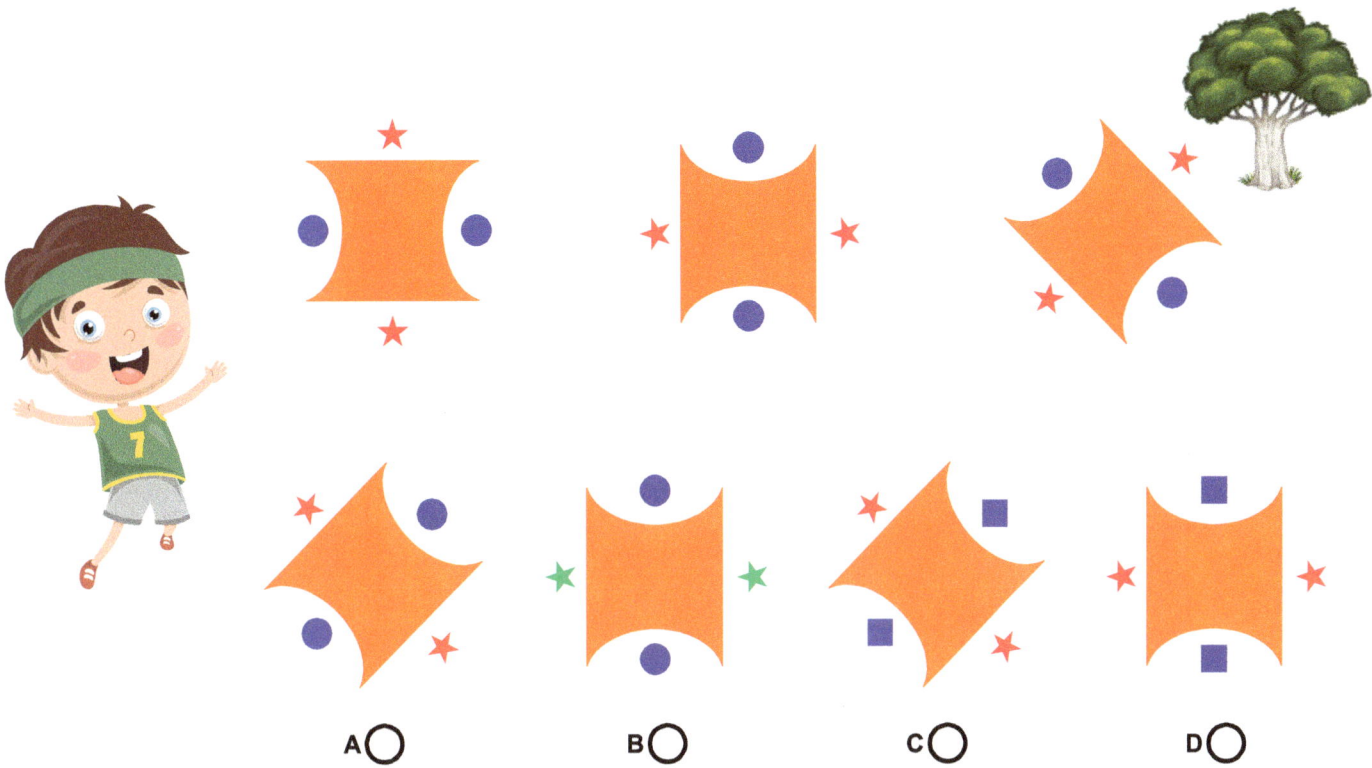

A◯   B◯   C◯   D◯

Solution : A

Option A is the only right choice. Option A matches the rest of the figure group in the same way. The other option vary in some way. Pay attention to all options before answering the right choice.

©All rights reserved-Math-Knots LLC., VA-USA

Q-1 Look at the question with the Raccoon. The first three pictures belong to one group in a common way. Help Jacob to find out which of the below options belong to the same group. Identify the correct picture and help him to bubble the right choice.

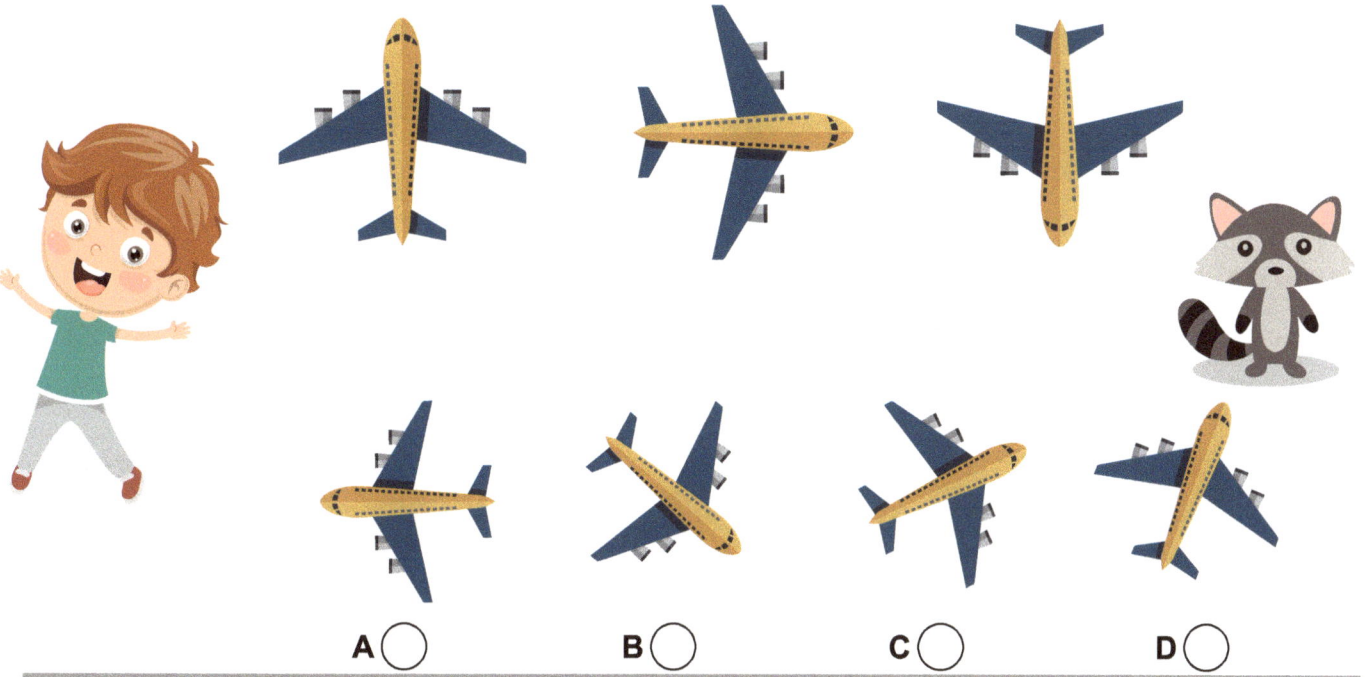

A◯   B◯   C◯   D◯

Q-2 Look at the question with the Walrus. The first three pictures belong to one group in a common way. Help Emma to find out which of the below options belong to the same group. Identify the correct picture and help her to bubble the right choice.

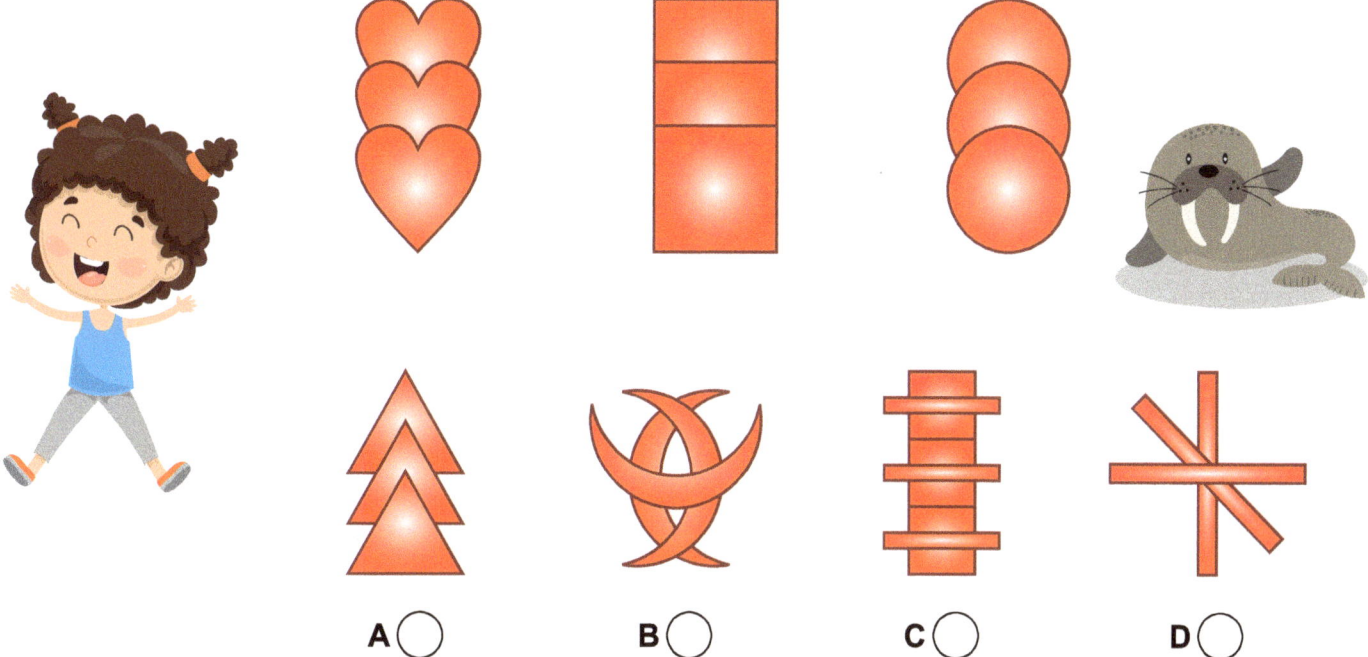

A◯   B◯   C◯   D◯

©All rights reserved-Math-Knots LLC., VA-USA

www.math-knots.com

Q-3

Look at the question with the Quail. The first three pictures belong to one group in a common way. Help Michael to find out which of the below options belong to the same group. Identify the correct picture and help him to bubble the right choice.

A ◯   B ◯   C ◯   D ◯

Q-4

Look at the question with the Jellyfish. The first three pictures belong to one group in a common way. Help Olivia to find out which of the below options belong to the same group. Identify the correct picture and help her to bubble the right choice.

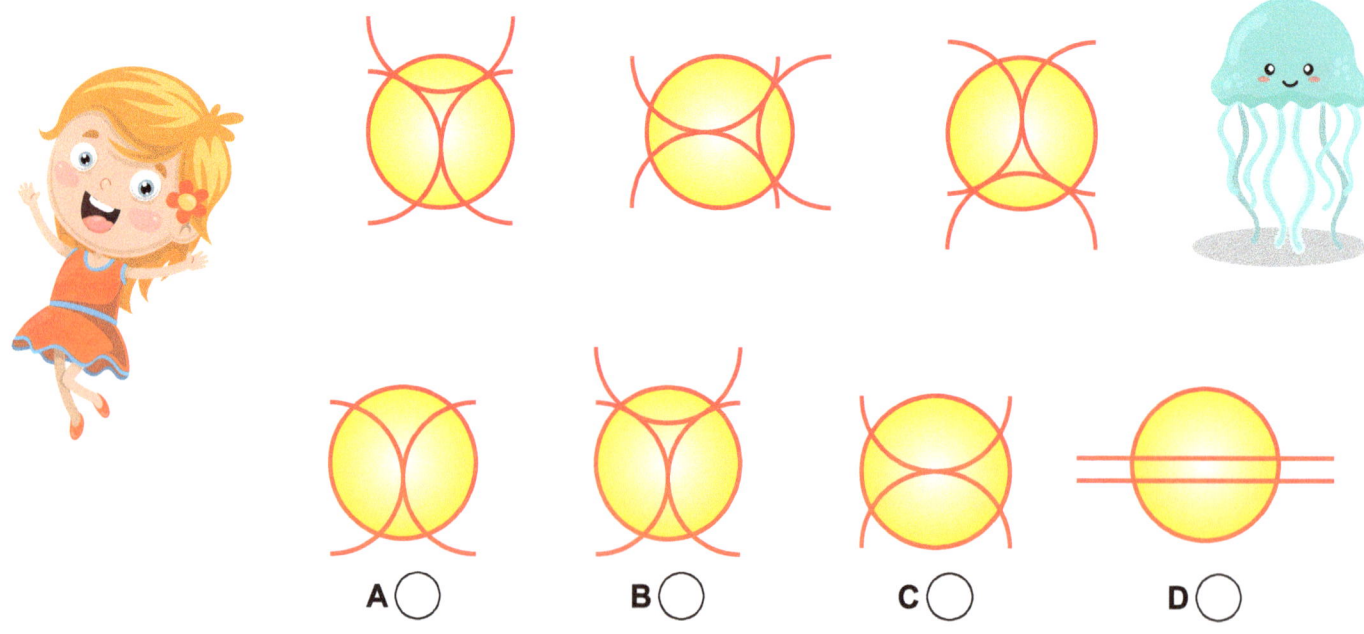

A ◯   B ◯   C ◯   D ◯

©All rights reserved-Math-Knots LLC., VA-USA

Q-5

Look at the question with the Elephant. The first three pictures belong to one group in a common way. Help Matthew to find out which of the below options belong to the same group. Identify the correct picture and help him to bubble the right choice.

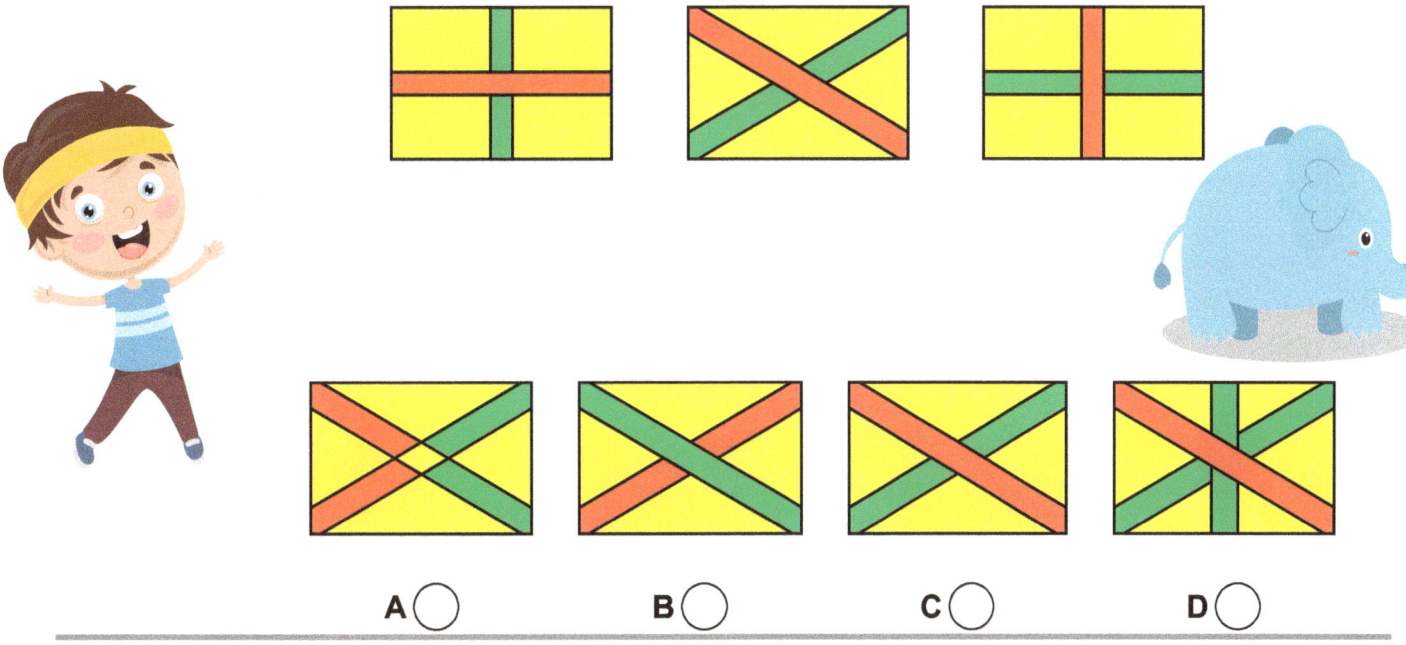

A ○   B ○   C ○   D ○

Q-6

Look at the question with the Turtle. The first three pictures belong to one group in a common way. Help Sophia to find out which of the below options belong to the same group. Identify the correct picture and help her to bubble the right choice.

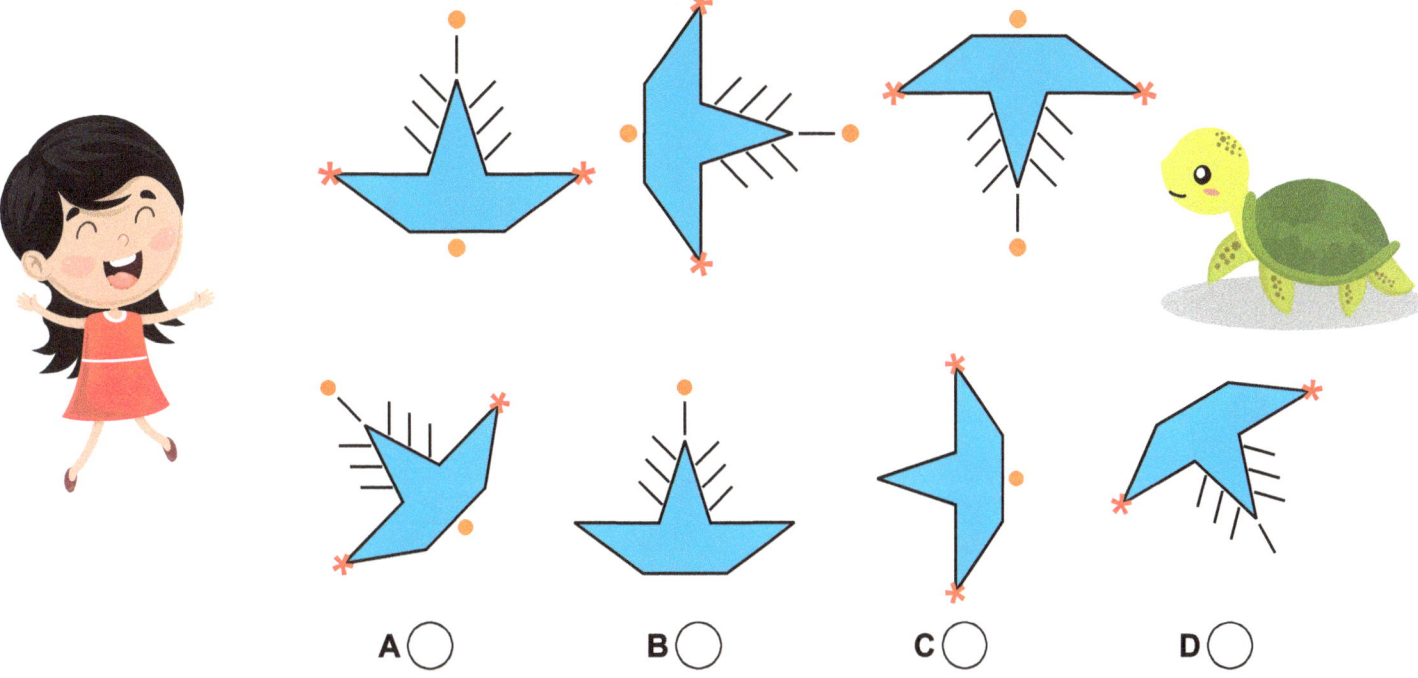

A ○   B ○   C ○   D ○

Q-7

Look at the question with the Monkey. The first three pictures belong to one group in a common way. Help Ethan to find out which of the below options belong to the same group. Identify the correct picture and help him to bubble the right choice.

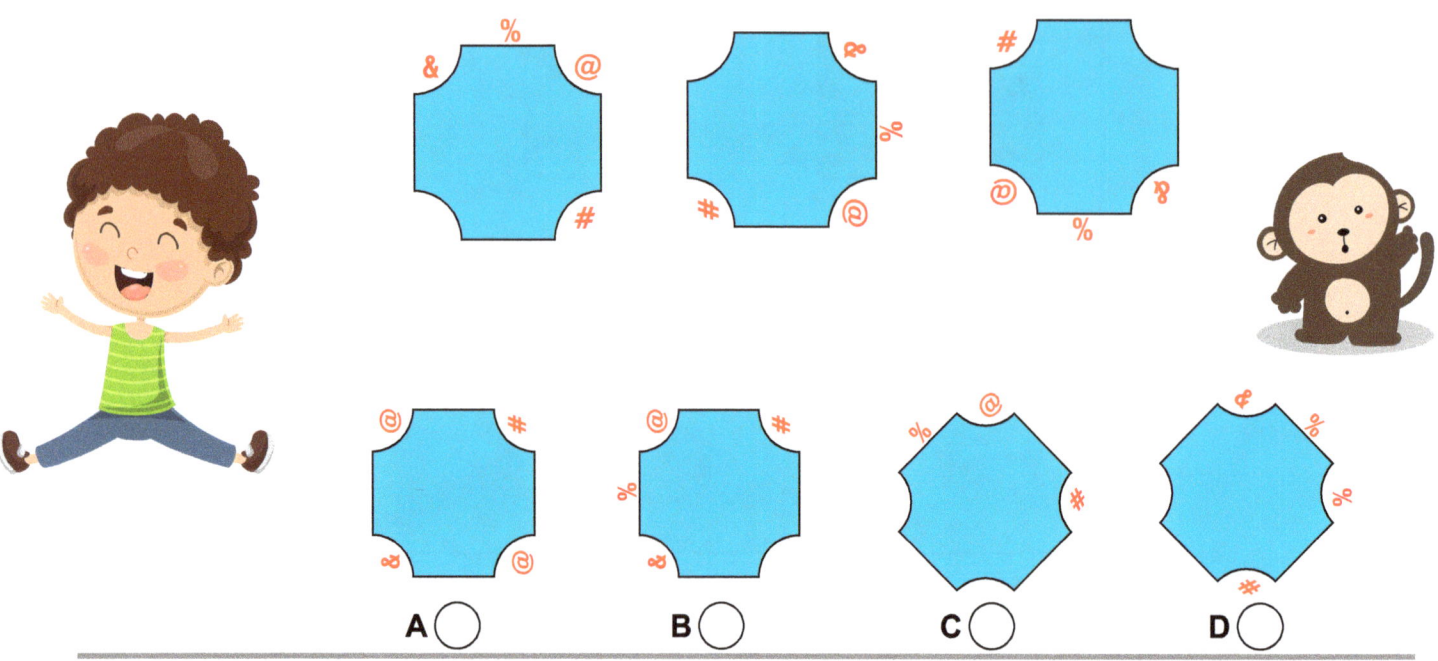

A ◯ B ◯ C ◯ D ◯

Q-8

Look at the question with the Narwhal Fish. The first three pictures belong to one group in a common way. Help Elizabeth to find out which of the below options belong to the same group. Identify the correct picture and help her to bubble the right choice.

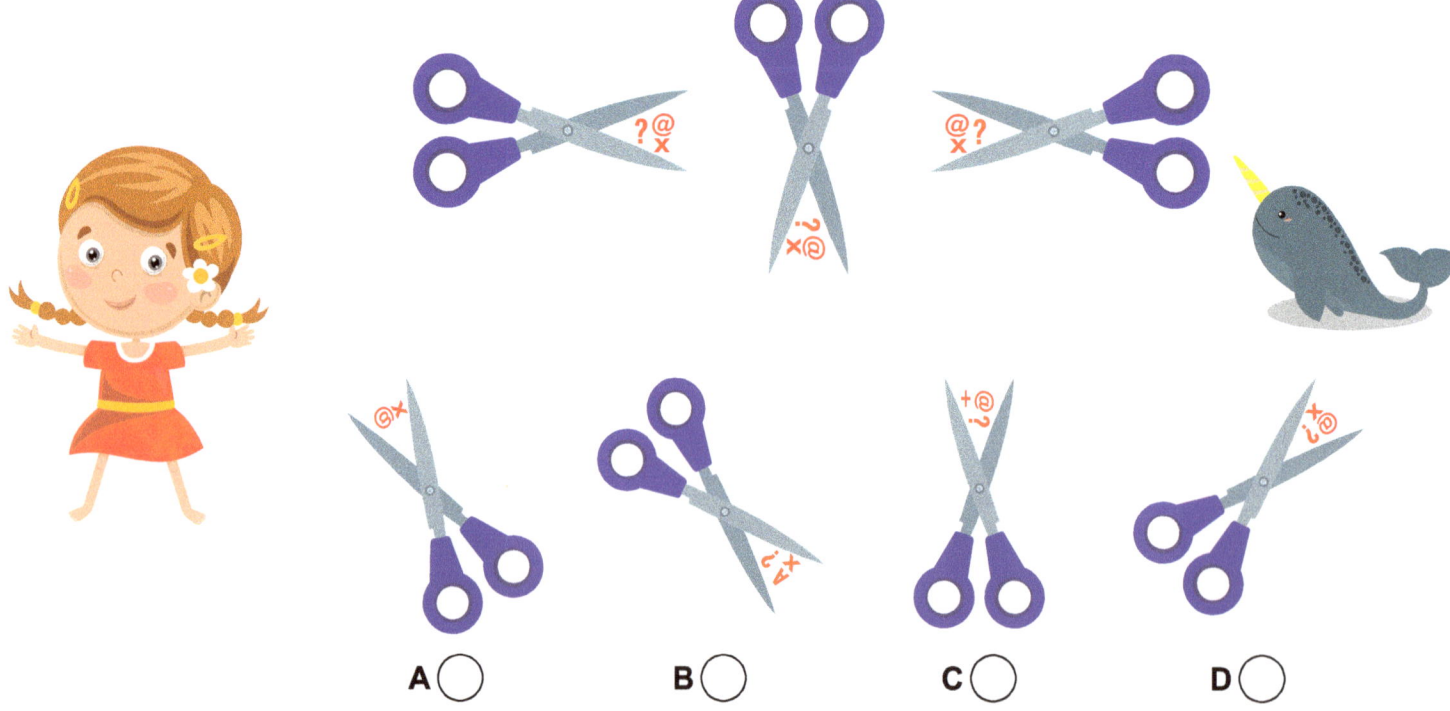

A ◯ B ◯ C ◯ D ◯

©All rights reserved-Math-Knots LLC., VA-USA
www.math-knots.com

Q-9

Look at the question with the Koala Bear. The first three pictures belong to one group in a common way. Help Andrew to find out which of the below options belong to the same group. Identify the correct picture and help him to bubble the right choice.

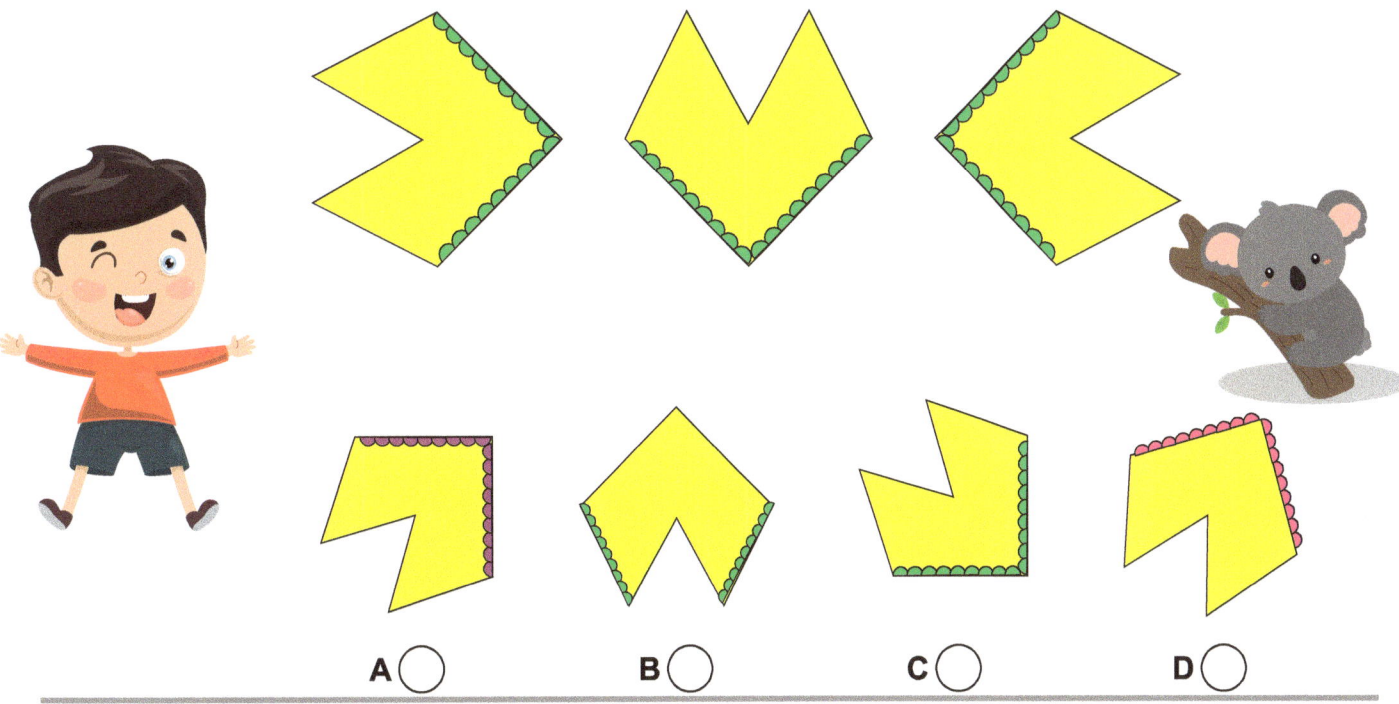

A ◯   B ◯   C ◯   D ◯

Q-10

Look at the question with the Lion. The first three pictures belong to one group in a common way. Help Jessica to find out which of the below options belong to the same group. Identify the correct picture and help her to bubble the right choice.

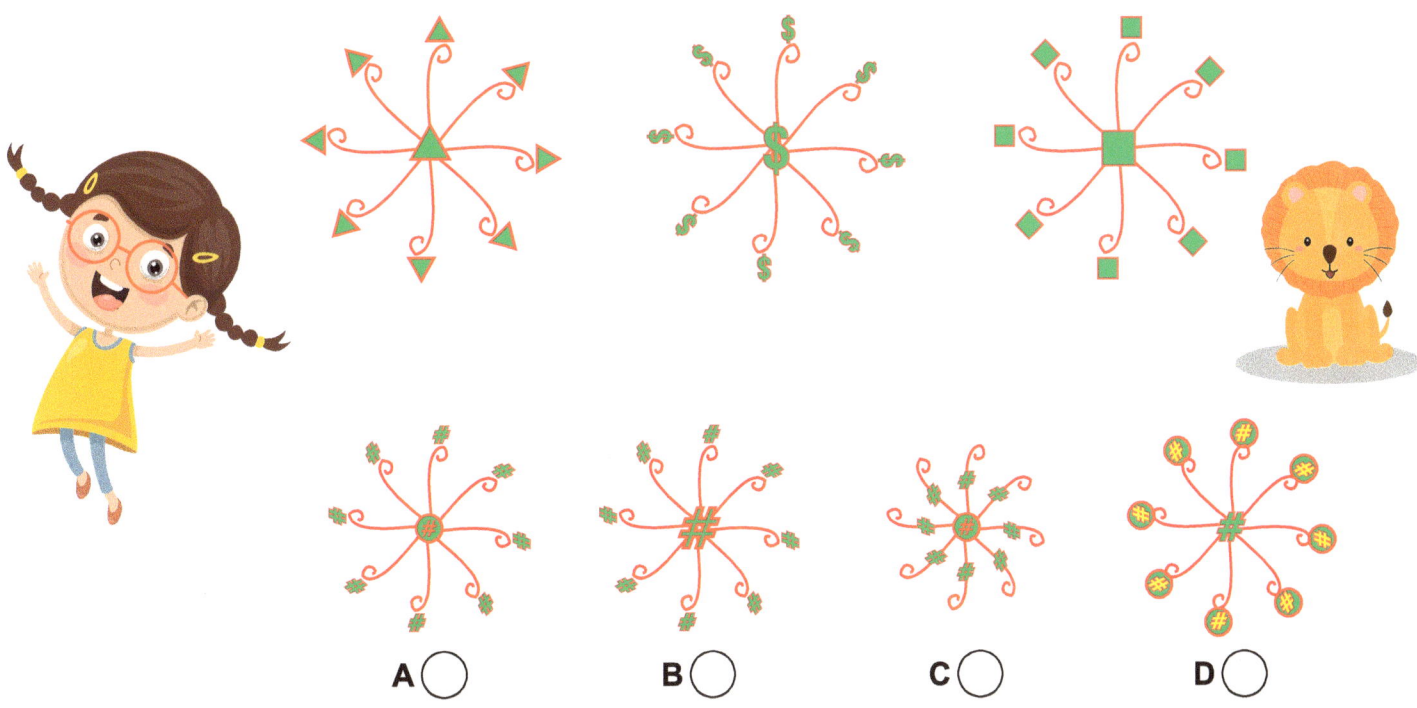

A ◯   B ◯   C ◯   D ◯

Q-11

Look at the question with the Iguana. The first three pictures belong to one group in a common way. Help Daniel to find out which of the below options belong to the same group. Identify the correct picture and help him to bubble the right choice.

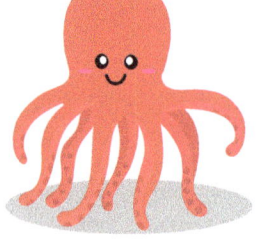

A ◯ B ◯ C ◯ D ◯

Q-12

Look at the question with the Octopus. The first three pictures belong to one group in a common way. Help Julia to find out which of the below options belong to the same group. Identify the correct picture and help her to bubble the right choice.

A ◯ B ◯ C ◯ D ◯

Q-13 Look at the question with the Dolphin. The first three pictures belong to one group in a common way. Help Anthony to find out which of the below options belong to the same group. Identify the correct picture and help him to bubble the right choice.

4 X 2   6 Y 4   8 P 6

10 P 8   7 P 5   5 K 1   9 S 6
A ◯   B ◯   C ◯   D ◯

Q-14 Look at the question with the Hedgehog. The first three pictures belong to one group in a common way. Help Jenna to find out which of the below options belong to the same group. Identify the correct picture and help her to bubble the right choice.

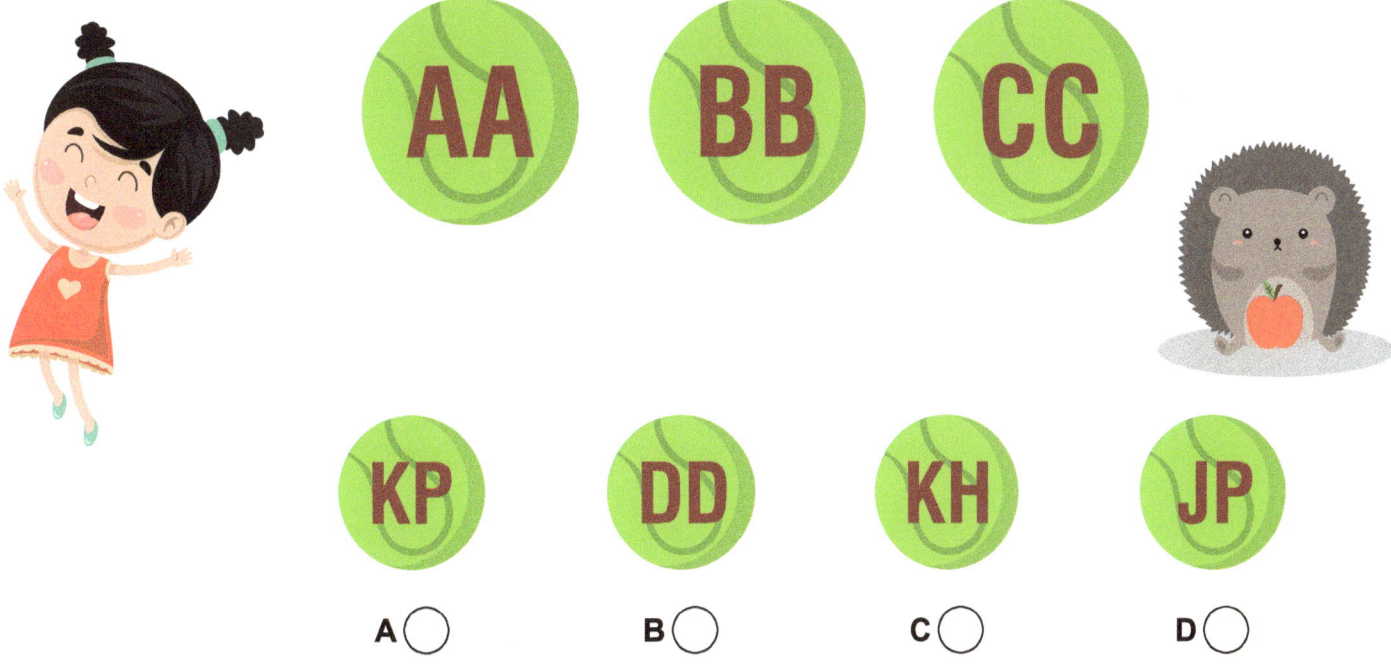

AA   BB   CC

KP   DD   KH   JP
A ◯   B ◯   C ◯   D ◯

©All rights reserved-Math-Knots LLC., VA-USA
www.math-knots.com

Q-15

Look at the question with the Fox. The first three pictures belong to one group in a common way. Help William to find out which of the below options belong to the same group. Identify the correct picture and help him to bubble the right choice.

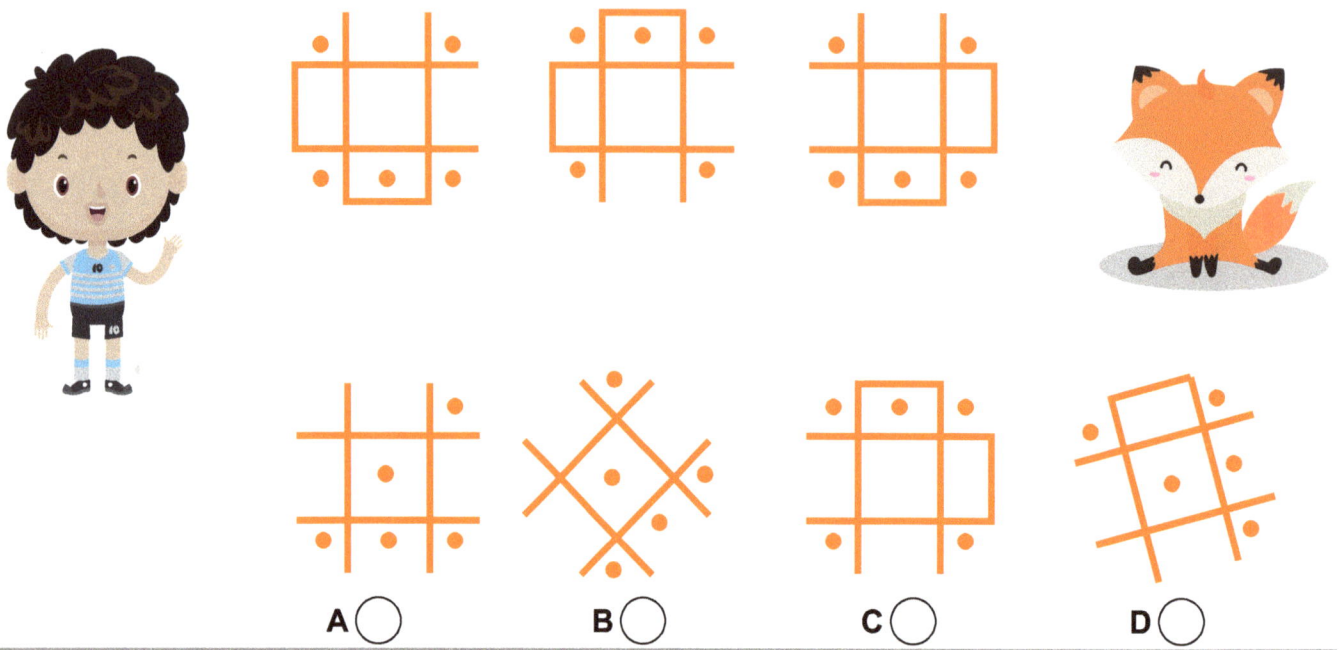

A◯   B◯   C◯   D◯

Q-16

Look at the question with the Giraffe. The first three pictures belong to one group in a common way. Help Mary to find out which of the below options belong to the same group. Identify the correct picture and help her to bubble the right choice.

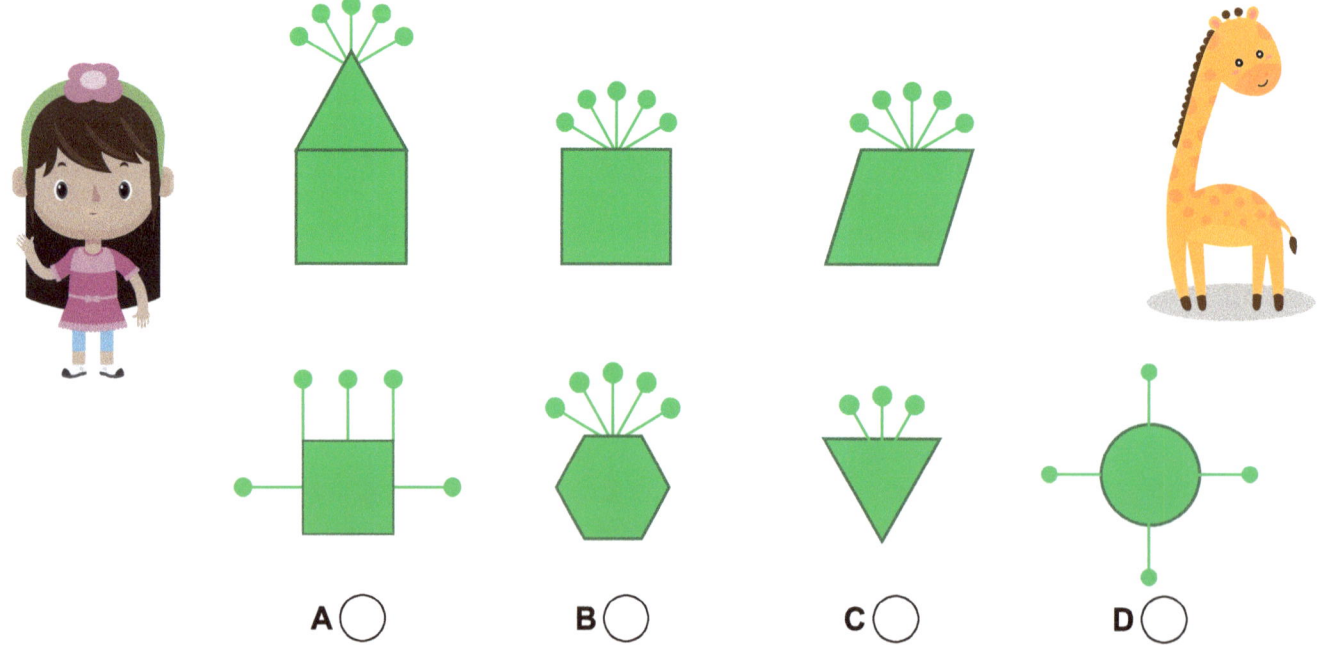

A◯   B◯   C◯   D◯

©All rights reserved-Math-Knots LLC., VA-USA
www.math-knots.com

Q-17

Look at the question with the Alligator. The first three pictures belong to one group in a common way. Help David to find out which of the below options belong to the same group. Identify the correct picture and help him to bubble the right choice.

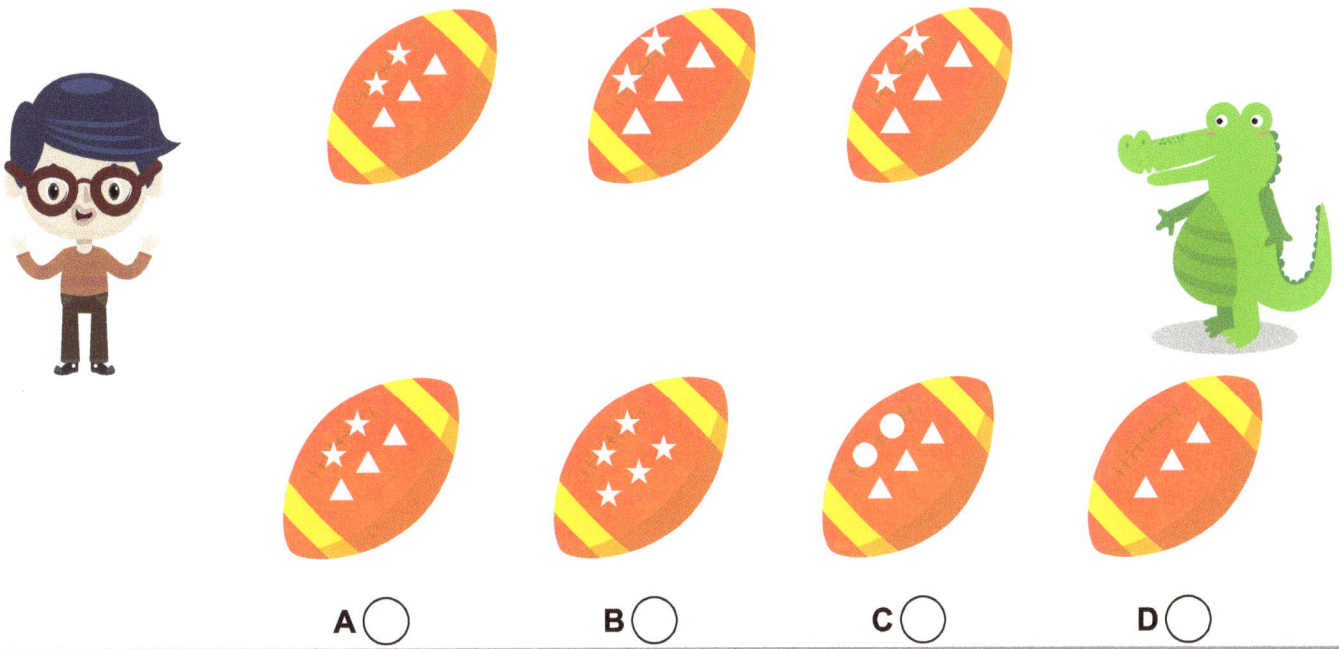

A ◯   B ◯   C ◯   D ◯

Q-18

Look at the question with the Bird. The first three pictures belong to one group in a common way. Help Amy to find out which of the below options belong to the same group. Identify the correct picture and help her to bubble the right choice.

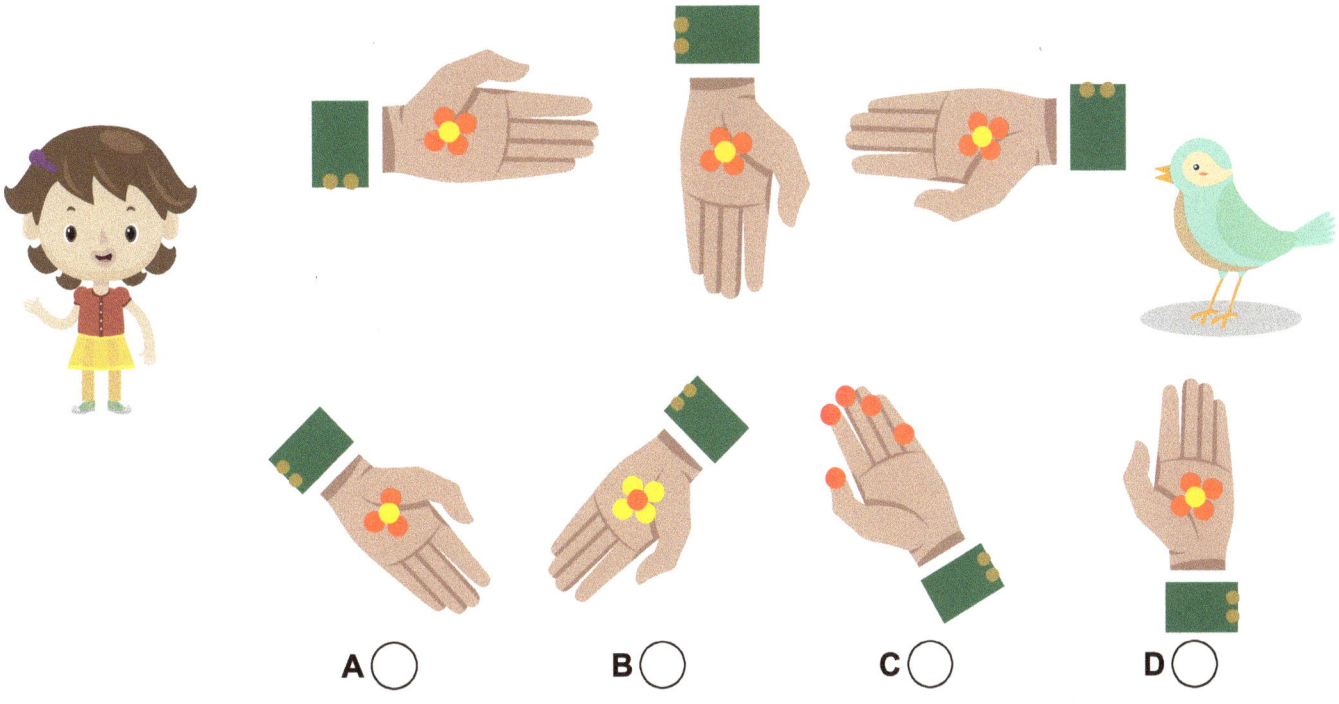

A ◯   B ◯   C ◯   D ◯

©All rights reserved-Math-Knots LLC., VA-USA
www.math-knots.com

©All rights reserved-Math-Knots LLC., VA-USA

TEST - 1

NON VERBAL SECTION

FIGURE MATRICES

Lets Start the Test...

©All rights reserved-Math-Knots LLC., VA-USA www.math-knots.com

©All rights reserved-Math-Knots LLC., VA-USA

Sample

Look at the question with the Grapes. The first row has some thing in common as the second row. Can you help Mary to identify what goes in the space of the question mark from the four given options A, B, C, and D. Choose the correct option.

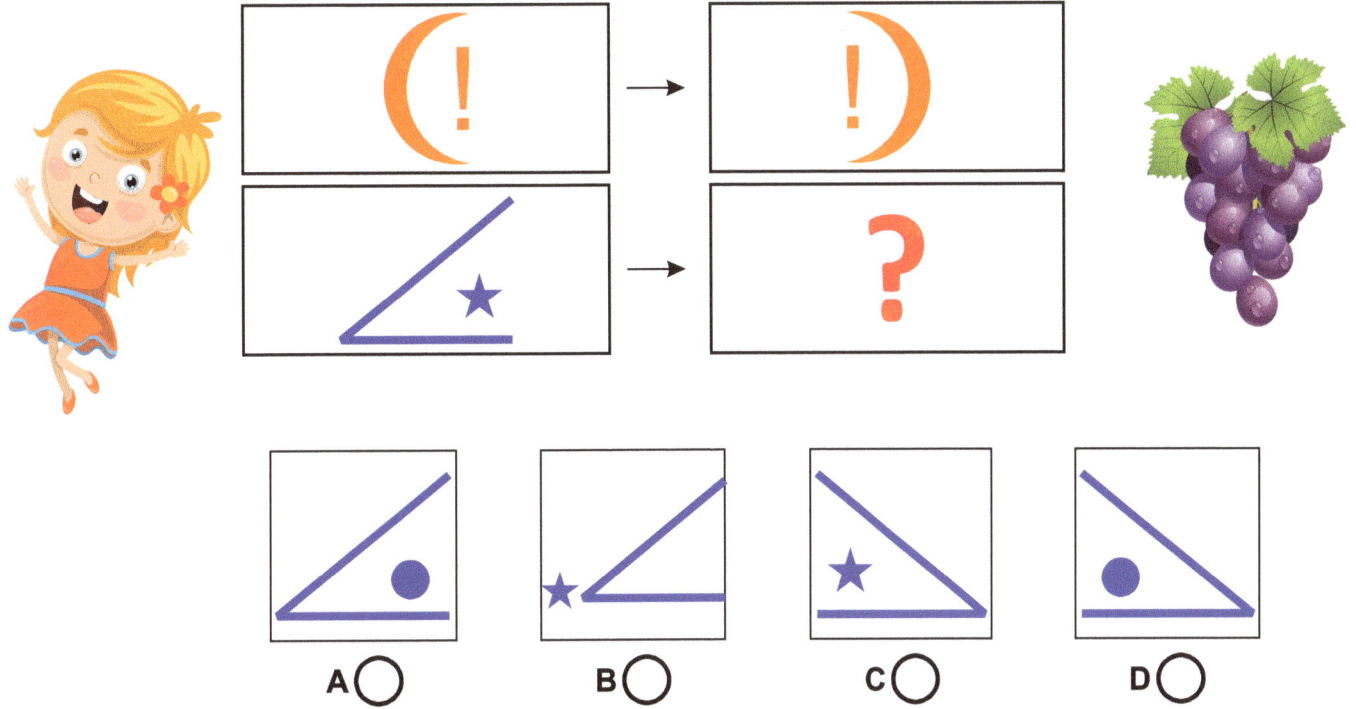

Solution : C

Option C is the right choice.

Two pictures in the first row are related in a certain way and the figures and flipped.

When the picture in the second row is flipped it will be match to option C.

Students need to pay attention. Figures can be turning clock wise into anti clock wise, and other possibilities.

©All rights reserved-Math-Knots LLC., VA-USA
www.math-knots.com

©All rights reserved-Math-Knots LLC., VA-USA

www.math-knots.com

Q-1

Look at the question with the Truck. The first row has some thing in common as the second row. Can you help Diana to identify what goes in the space of the question mark from the four given options A, B, C, and D. Choose the correct option.

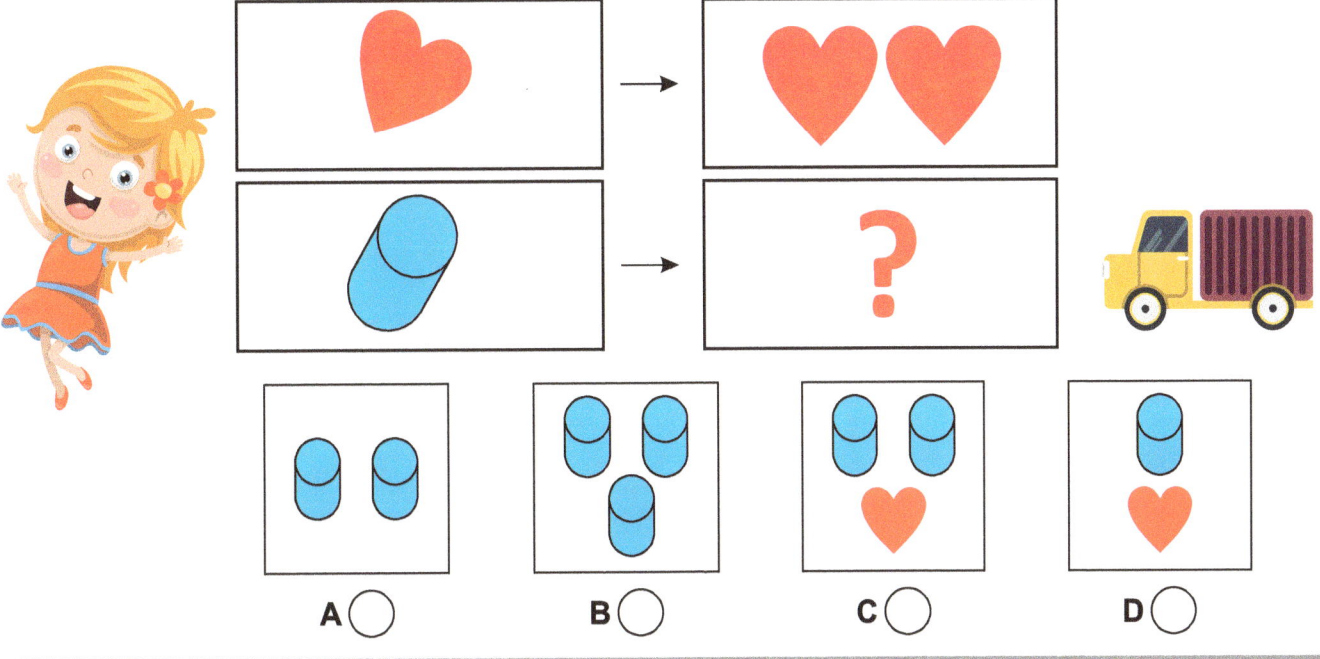

Q-2

Look at the question with the Mini Bus. The first row has some thing in common as the second row. Can you help Maria to identify what goes in the space of the question mark from the four given options A, B, C, and D. Choose the correct option.

Q-3

Look at the question with the Jeep. The first row has some thing in common as the second row. Can you help George to identify what goes in the space of the question mark from the four given options A, B, C, and D. Choose the correct option.

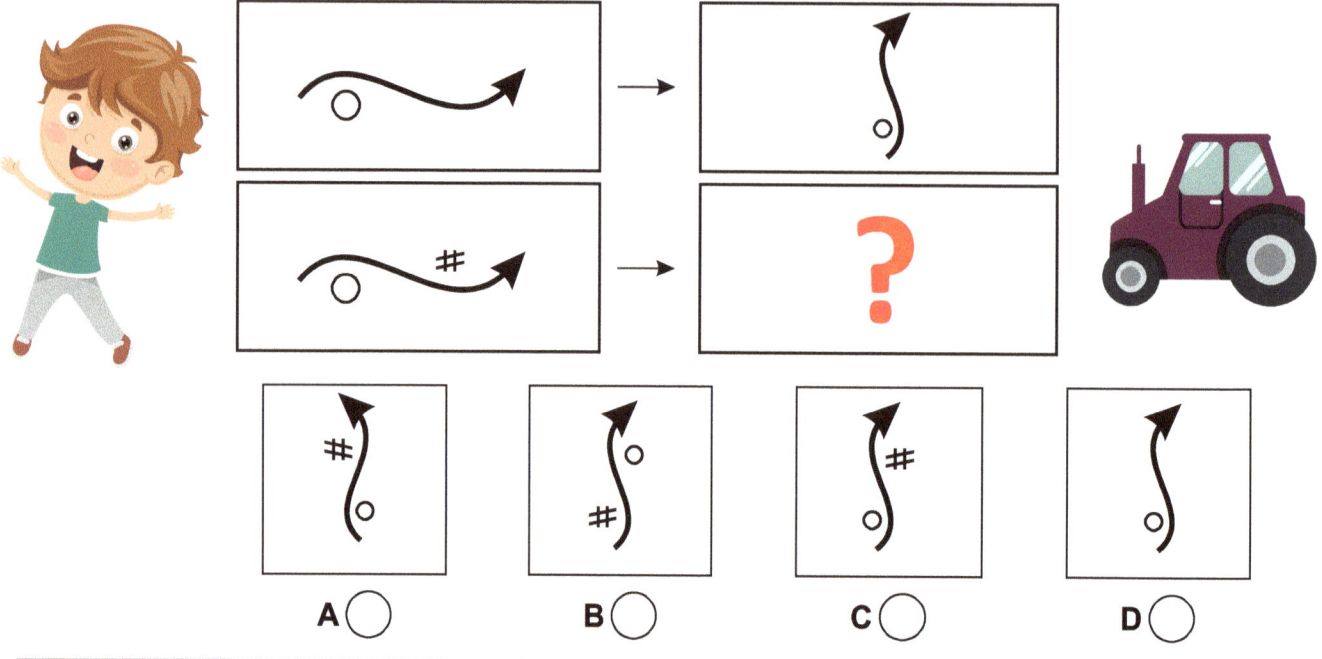

Q-4

Look at the question with the Train. The first row has some thing in common as the second row. Can you help Bryan to identify what goes in the space of the question mark from the four given options A, B, C, and D. Choose the correct option.

Q-5

Look at the question with the Oil Tanker. The first row has some thing in common as the second row. Can you help Ria to identify what goes in the space of the question mark from the four given options A, B, C, and D. Choose the correct option.

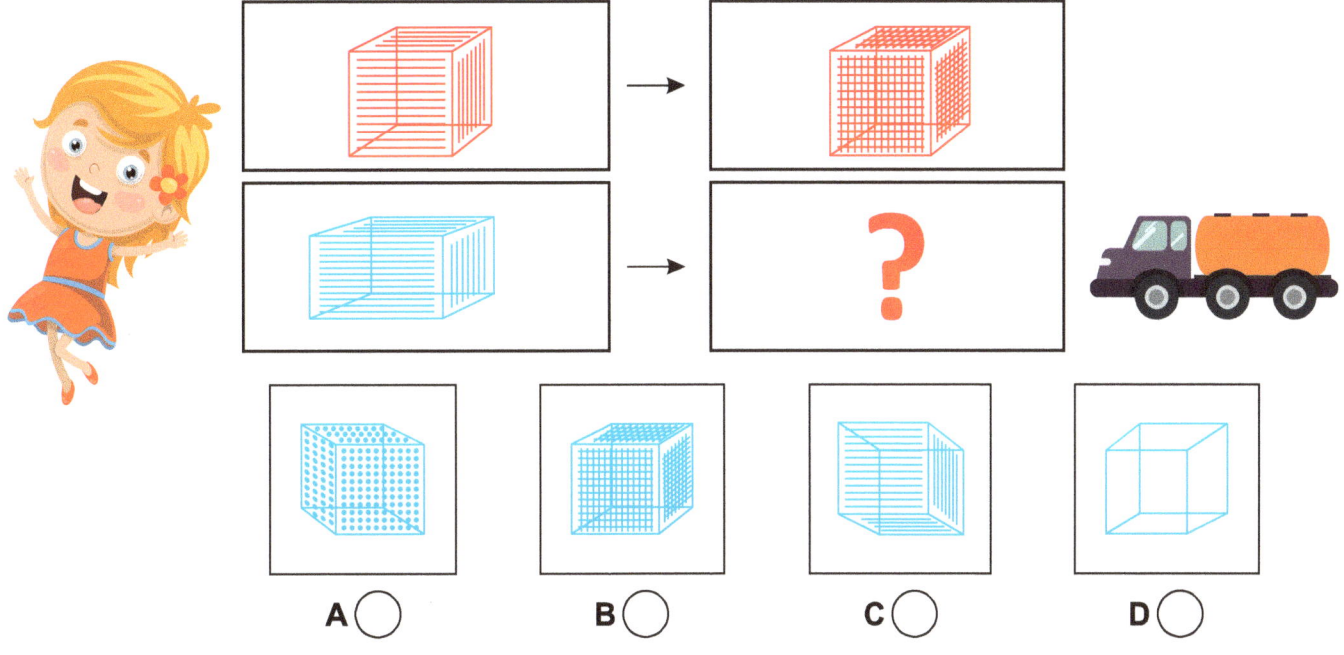

A ◯   B ◯   C ◯   D ◯

Q-6

Look at the question with the Ship. The first row has some thing in common as the second row. Can you help Julie to identify what goes in the space of the question mark from the four given options A, B, C, and D. Choose the correct option.

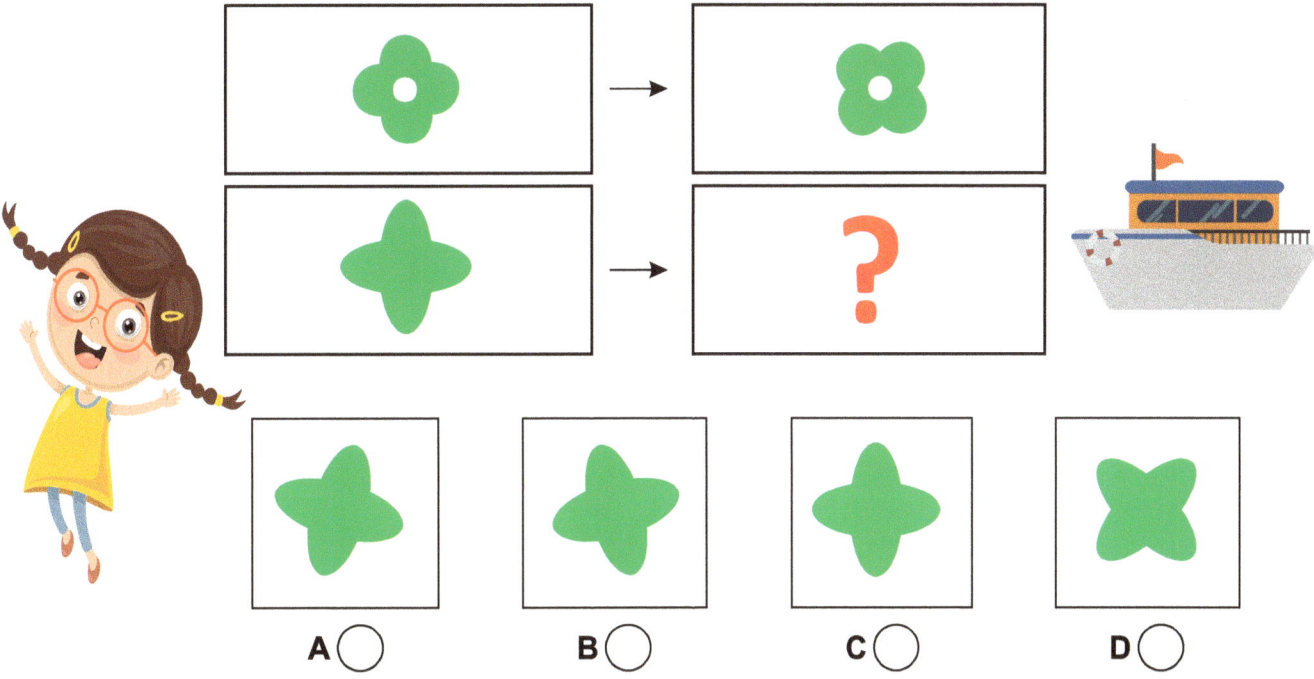

A ◯   B ◯   C ◯   D ◯

Q-7

Look at the question with the Fire Engine truck. The first row has some thing in common as the second row. Can you help Aryan to identify what goes in the space of the question mark from the four given options A, B, C, and D. Choose the correct option.

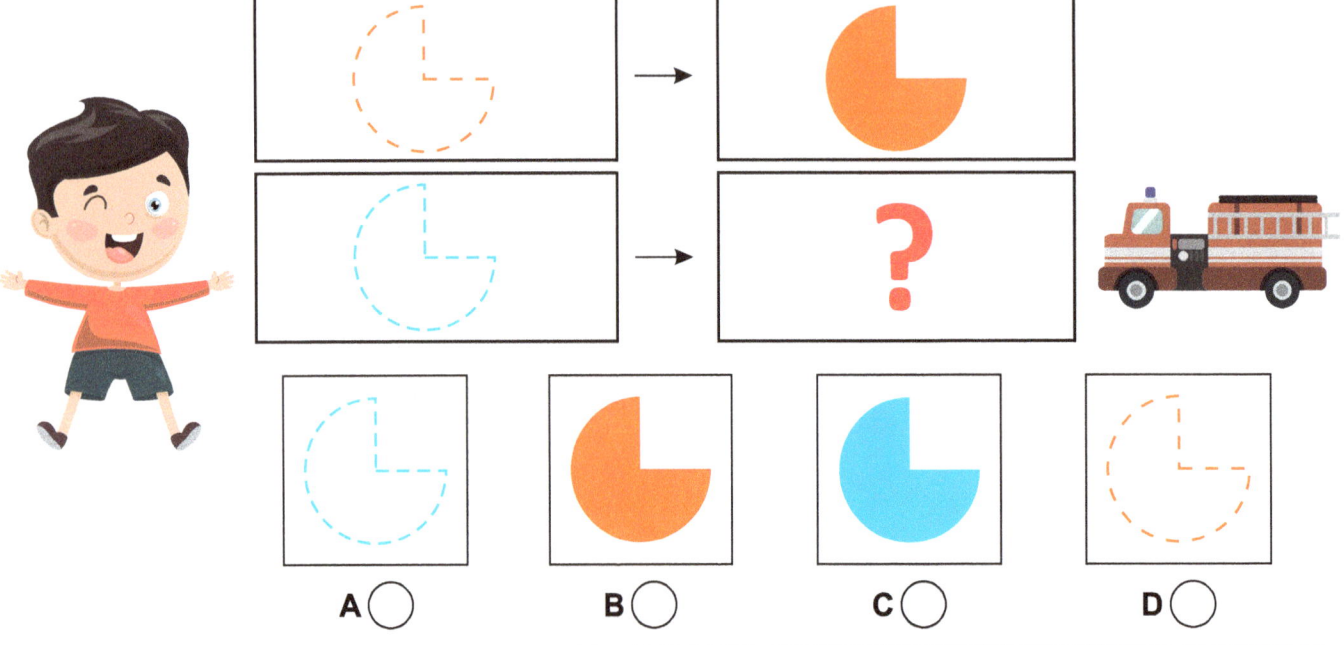

A ○   B ○   C ○   D ○

Q-8

Look at the question with the Crane. The first row has some thing in common as the second row. Can you help Mike to identify what goes in the space of the question mark from the four given options A, B, C, and D. Choose the correct option.

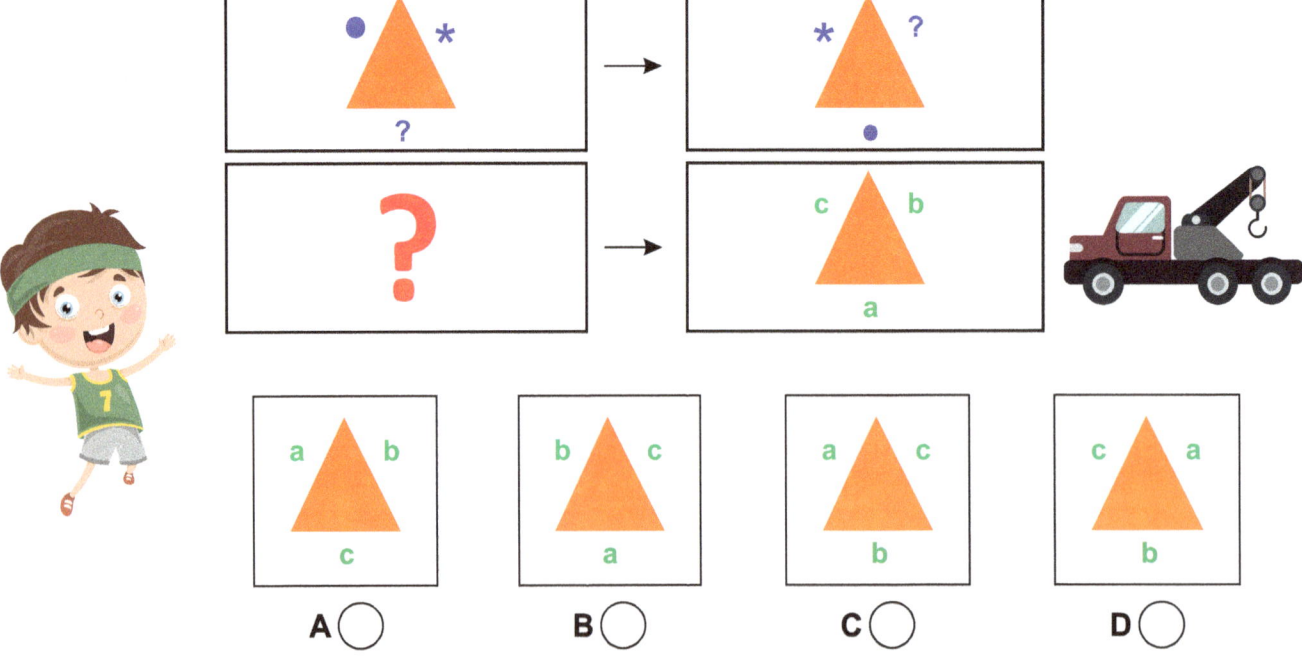

A ○   B ○   C ○   D ○

©All rights reserved-Math-Knots LLC., VA-USA
www.math-knots.com

Q-9

Look at the question with the Bus. The first row has some thing in common as the second row. Can you help Cathy to identify what goes in the space of the question mark from the four given options A, B, C, and D. Choose the correct option.

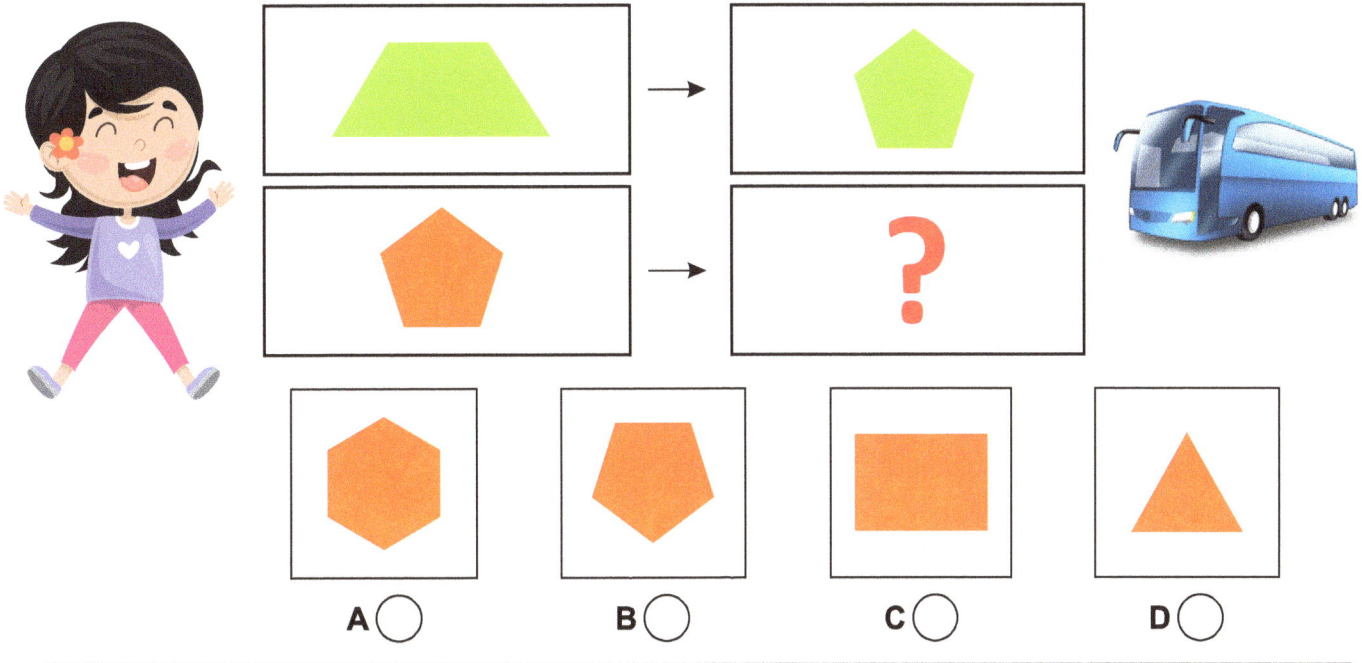

Q-10

Look at the question with the Scooter. The first row has some thing in common as the second row. Can you help Jason to identify what goes in the space of the question mark from the four given options A, B, C, and D. Choose the correct option.

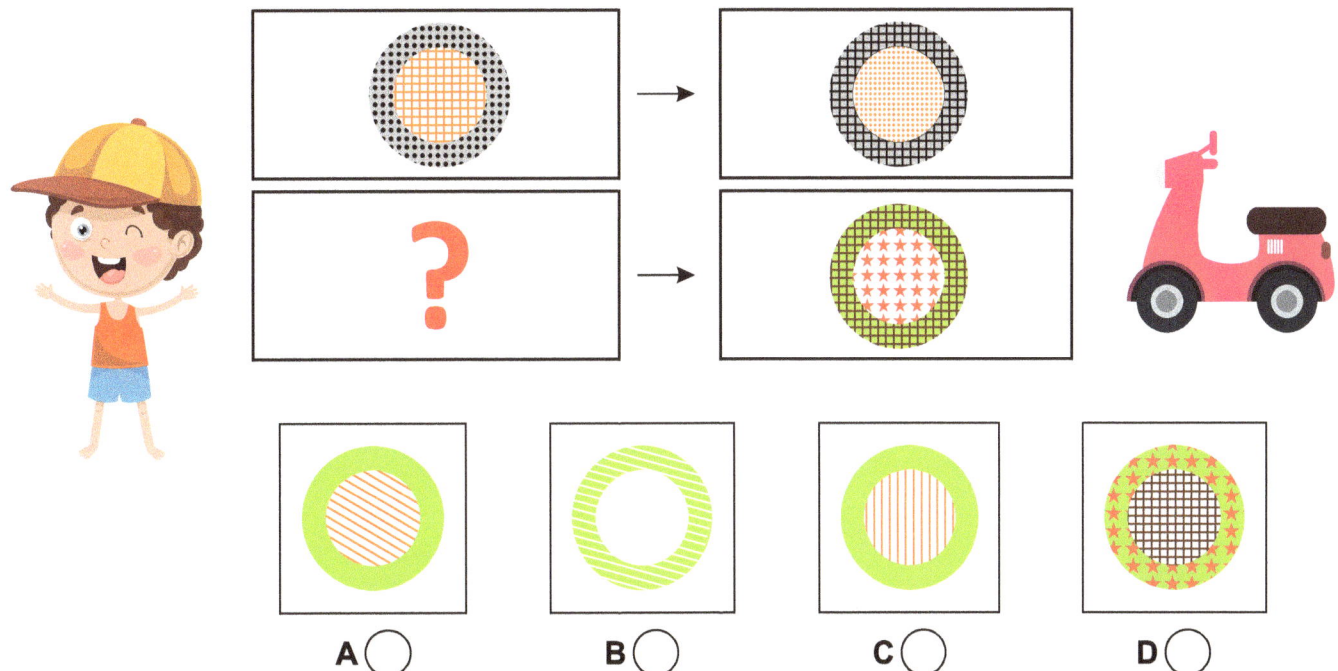

Q-11 Look at the question with the Bicycle. The first row has some thing in common as the second row. Can you help David to identify what goes in the space of the question mark from the four given options A, B, C, and D. Choose the correct option.

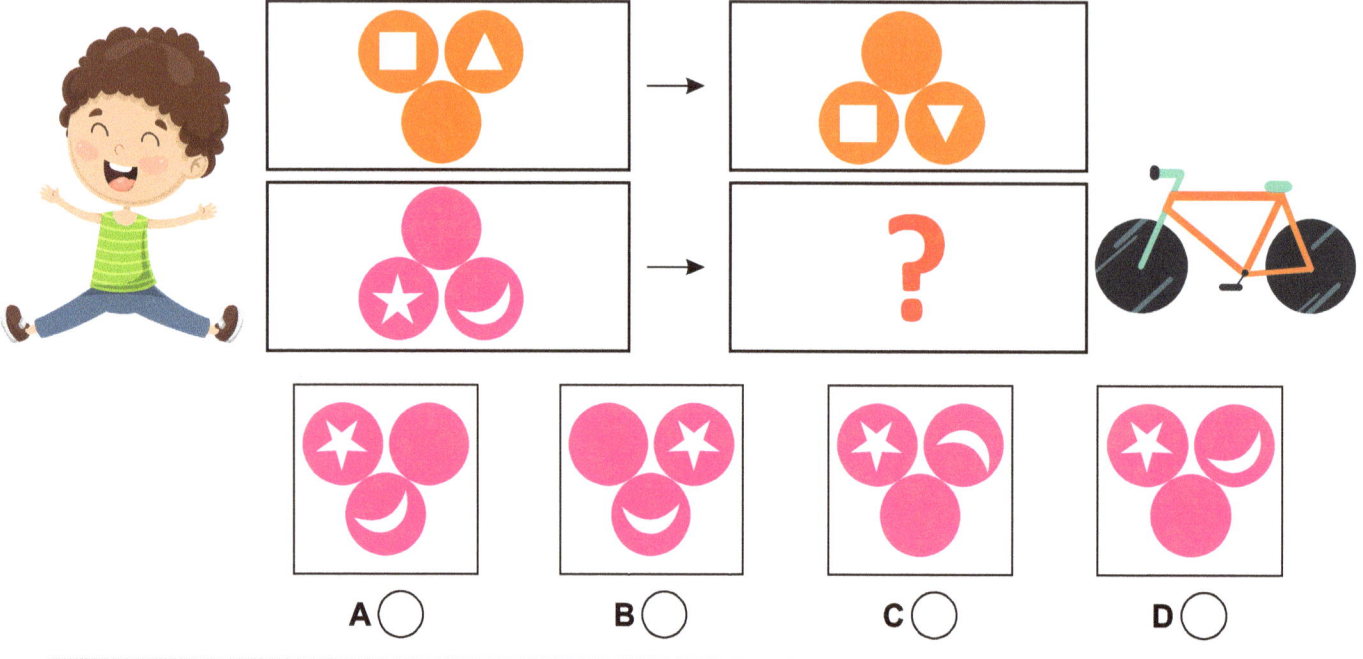

Q-12 Look at the question with the Hot Air Balloon. The first row has some thing in common as the second row. Can you help Mary to identify what goes in the space of the question mark from the four given options A, B, C, and D. Choose the correct option.

Q-13

Look at the question with the Car. The first row has some thing in common as the second row. Can you help Oscar to identify what goes in the space of the question mark from the four given options A, B, C, and D. Choose the correct option.

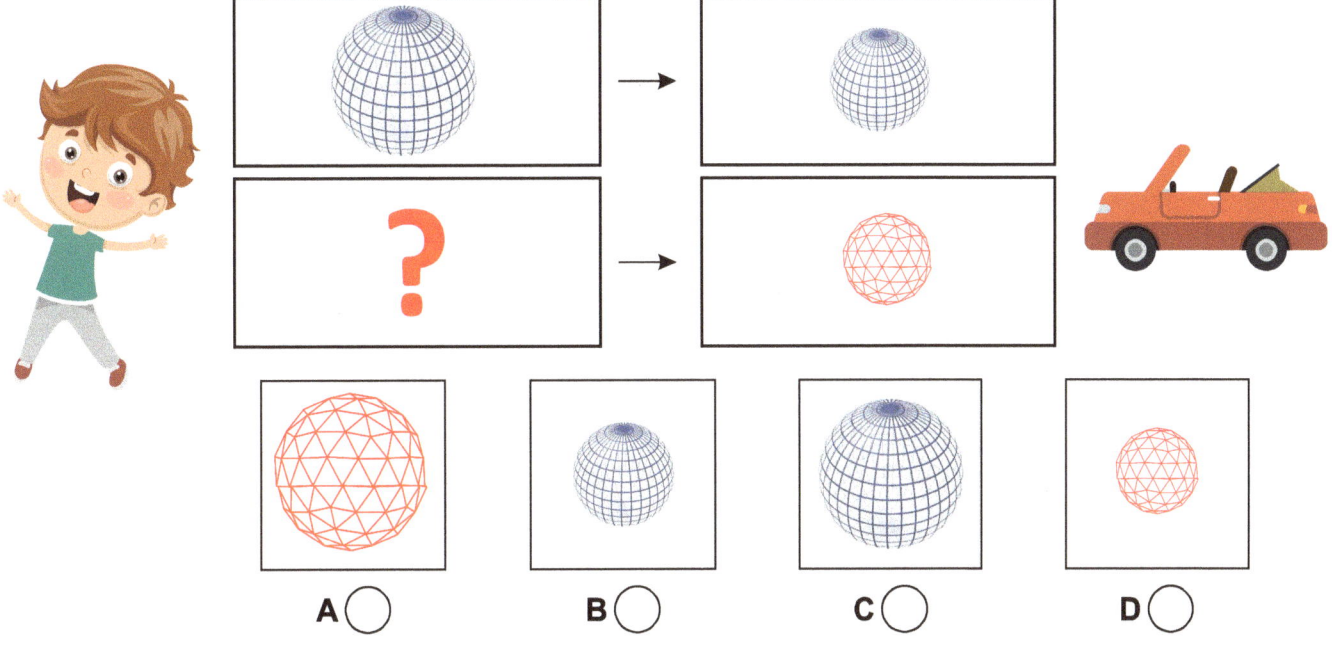

A ○   B ○   C ○   D ○

Q-14

Look at the question with the Cement Mixer. The first row has some thing in common as the second row. Can you help Grace to identify what goes in the space of the question mark from the four given options A, B, C, and D. Choose the correct option.

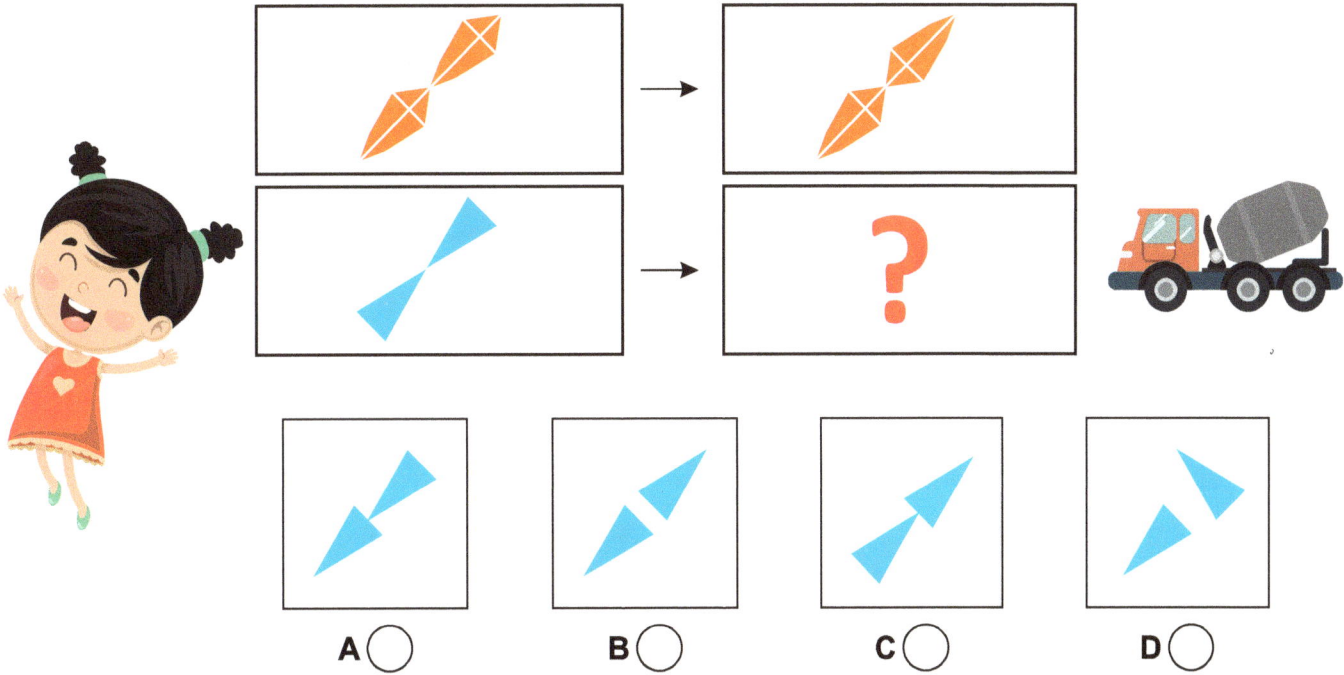

A ○   B ○   C ○   D ○

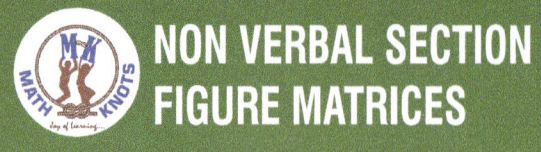

Q-15

Look at the question with the Mini Truck. The first row has some thing in common as the second row. Can you help Wesley to identify what goes in the space of the question mark from the four given options A, B, C, and D. Choose the correct option.

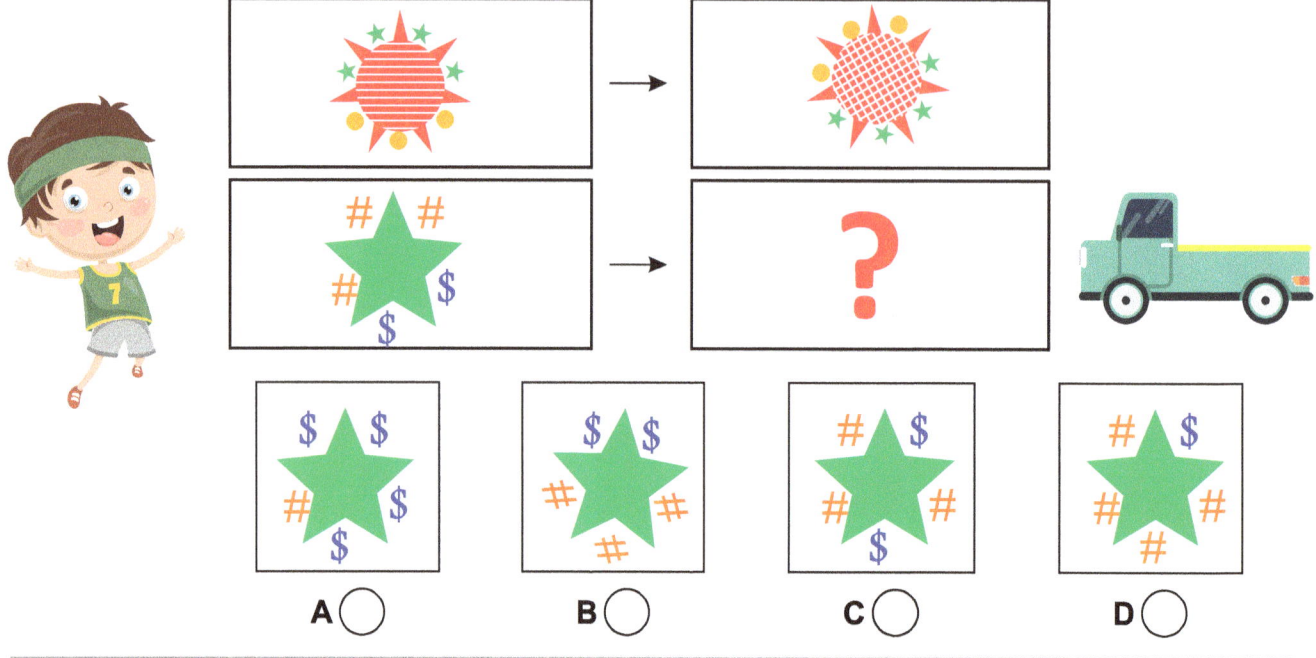

Q-16

Look at the question with the Helicopter. The first row has some thing in common as the second row. Can you help Jack to identify what goes in the space of the question mark from the four given options A, B, C, and D. Choose the correct option.

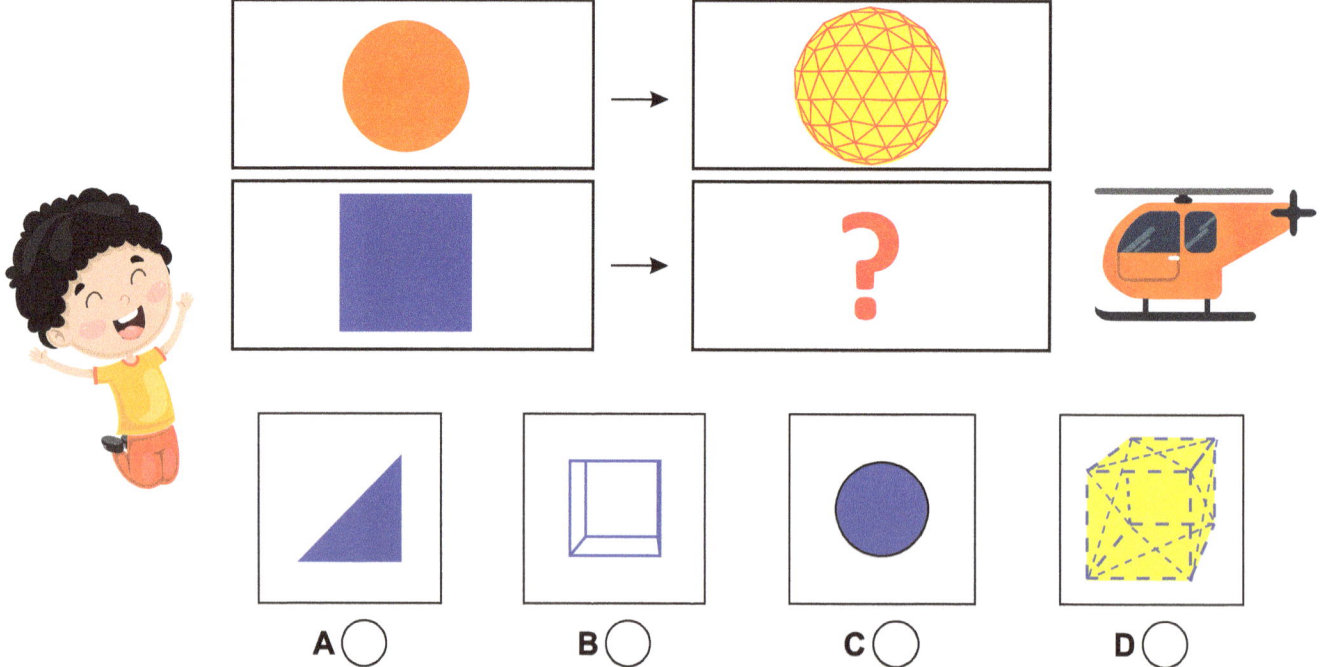

©All rights reserved-Math-Knots LLC., VA-USA

www.math-knots.com

Q-17

Look at the question with the Aeroplane. The first row has some thing in common as the second row. Can you help Owen to identify what goes in the space of the question mark from the four given options A, B, C, and D. Choose the correct option.

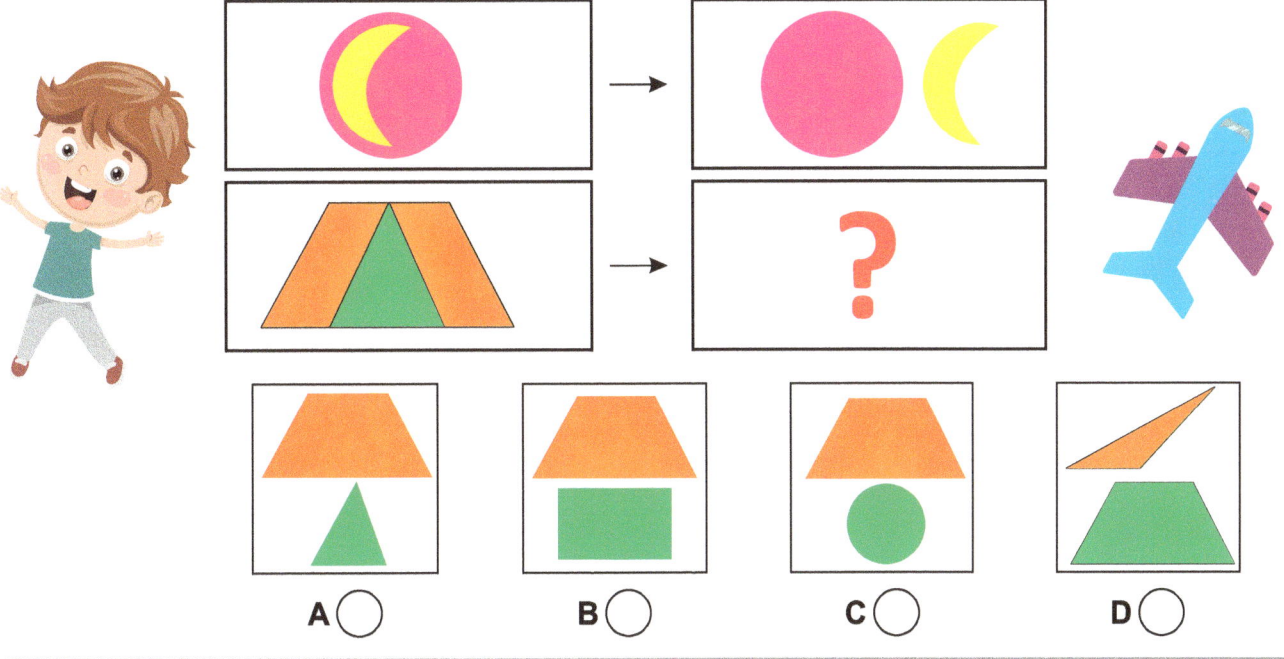

A ◯   B ◯   C ◯   D ◯

Q-18

Look at the question with the Ambulance. The first row has some thing in common as the second row. Can you help Rita to identify what goes in the space of the question mark from the four given options A, B, C, and D. Choose the correct option.

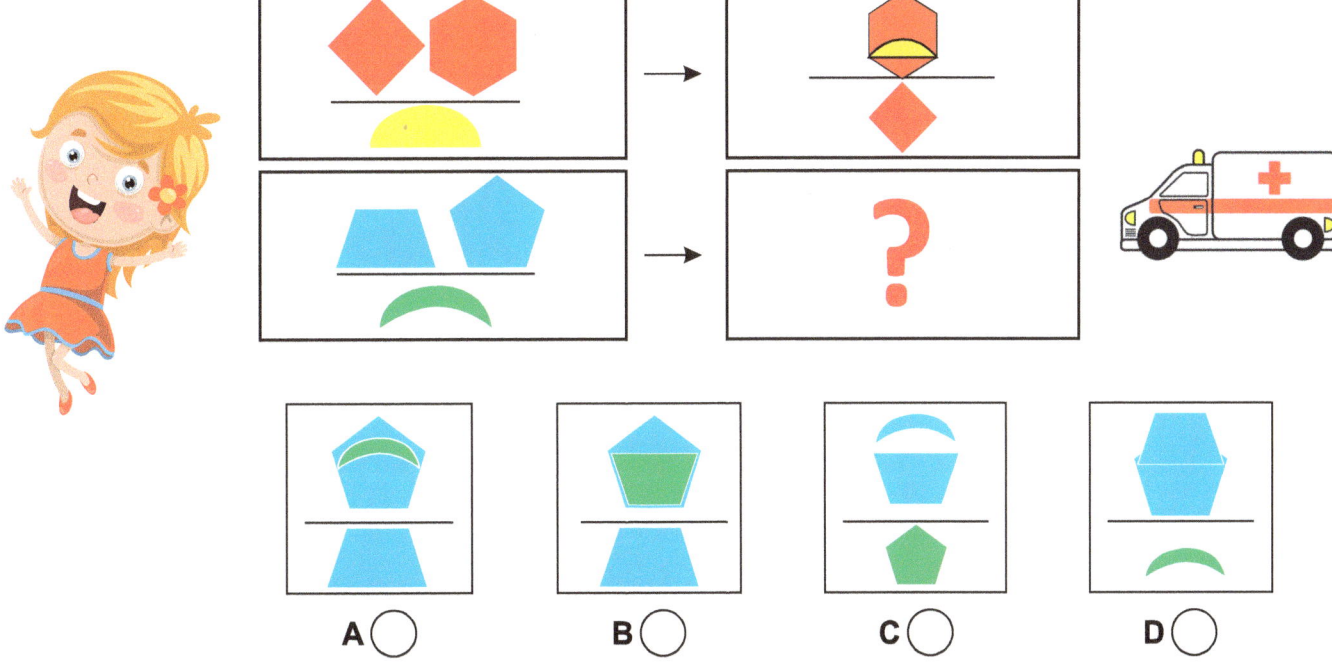

A ◯   B ◯   C ◯   D ◯

©All rights reserved-Math-Knots LLC., VA-USA

TEST - 1

NON VERBAL SECTION

PAPER FOLDING

Lets Start the Test...

©All rights reserved-Math-Knots LLC., VA-USA

www.math-knots.com

©All rights reserved-Math-Knots LLC., VA-USA

NON VERBAL SECTION
PAPER FOLDING

Sample Look at the question and put your finger on Bee. Amy folded the paper and made holes to it as shown. When the paper is unfolded how does it look? Help her bubble the right option.

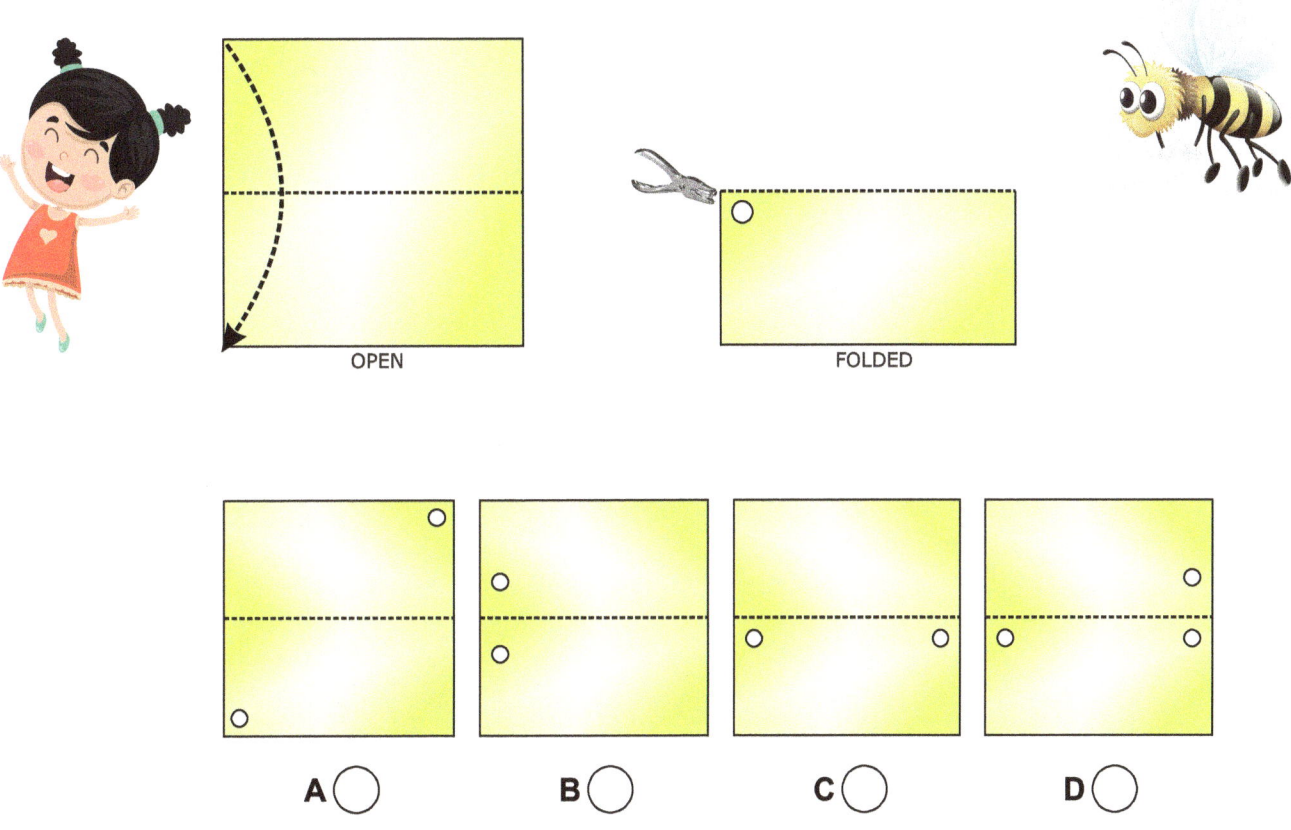

OPEN

FOLDED

A◯ B◯ C◯ D◯

Solution : B

A rectangle is folded once and hole is punched on top left corner. After punching the figure is unfolded the holes are shown in the middle left corner as shown in option B. Student choses the right option and fills the bubble completely.

©All rights reserved-Math-Knots LLC., VA-USA   119

©All rights reserved-Math-Knots LLC., VA-USA

Q-1

Look at the question and put your finger on Star. Jack folded the paper and made holes to it as shown. When the paper is unfolded how does it look? Help him bubble the right option.

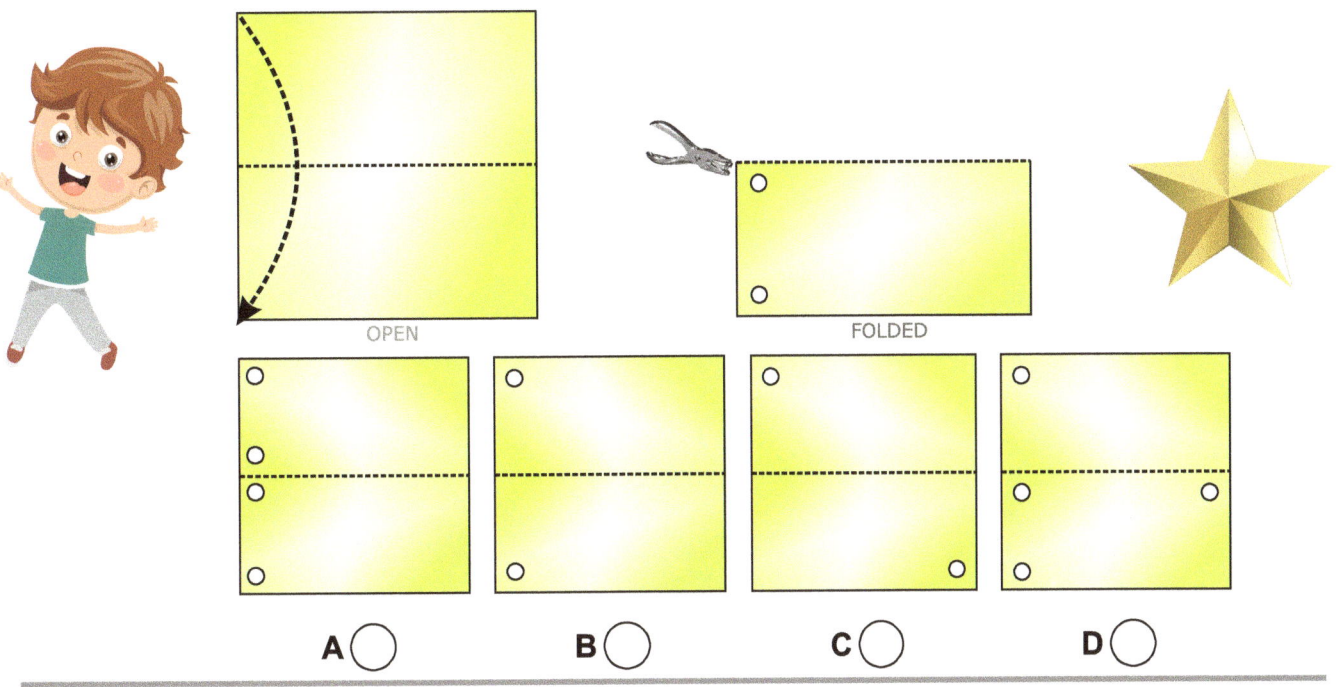

OPEN   FOLDED

A ◯   B ◯   C ◯   D ◯

Q-2

Look at the question and put your finger on Moon. Dora folded the paper and made holes to it as shown. When the paper is unfolded how does it look? Help her bubble the right option.

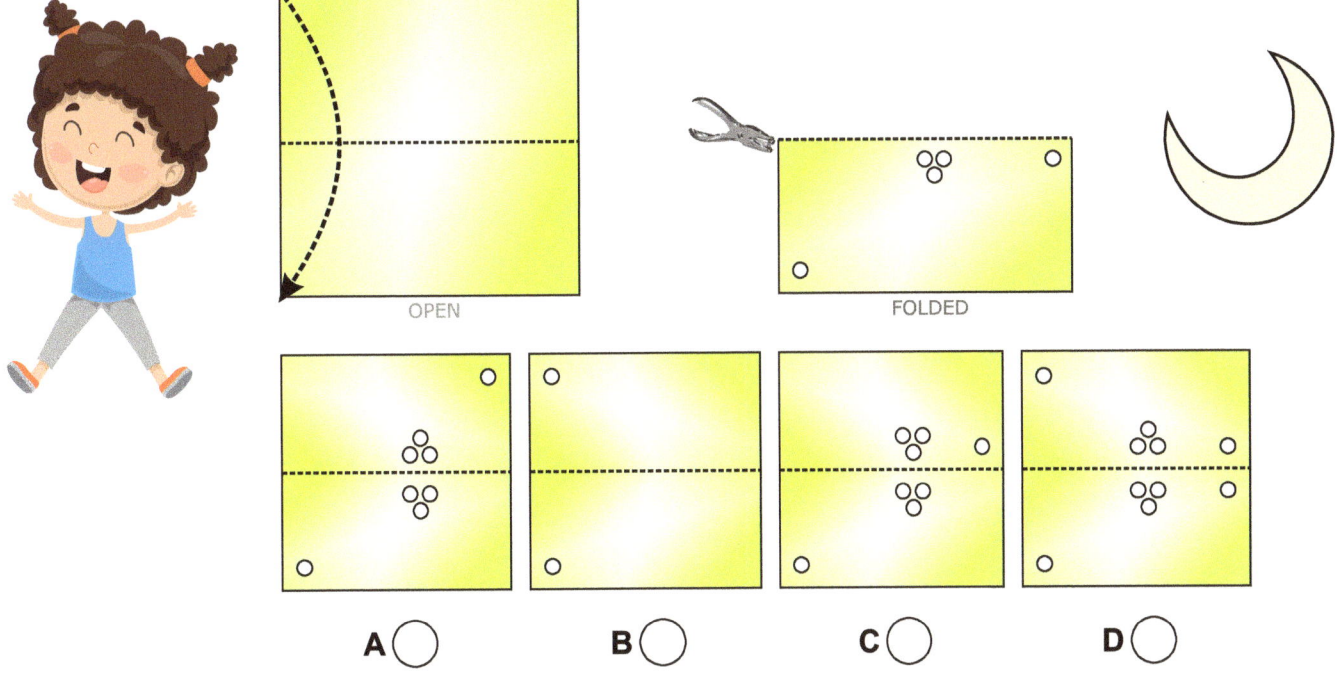

OPEN   FOLDED

A ◯   B ◯   C ◯   D ◯

©All rights reserved-Math-Knots LLC., VA-USA

www.math-knots.com

Q-3

Look at the question and put your finger on Sun. Johnson folded the paper and made holes to it as shown. When the paper is unfolded how does it look? Help him bubble the right option.

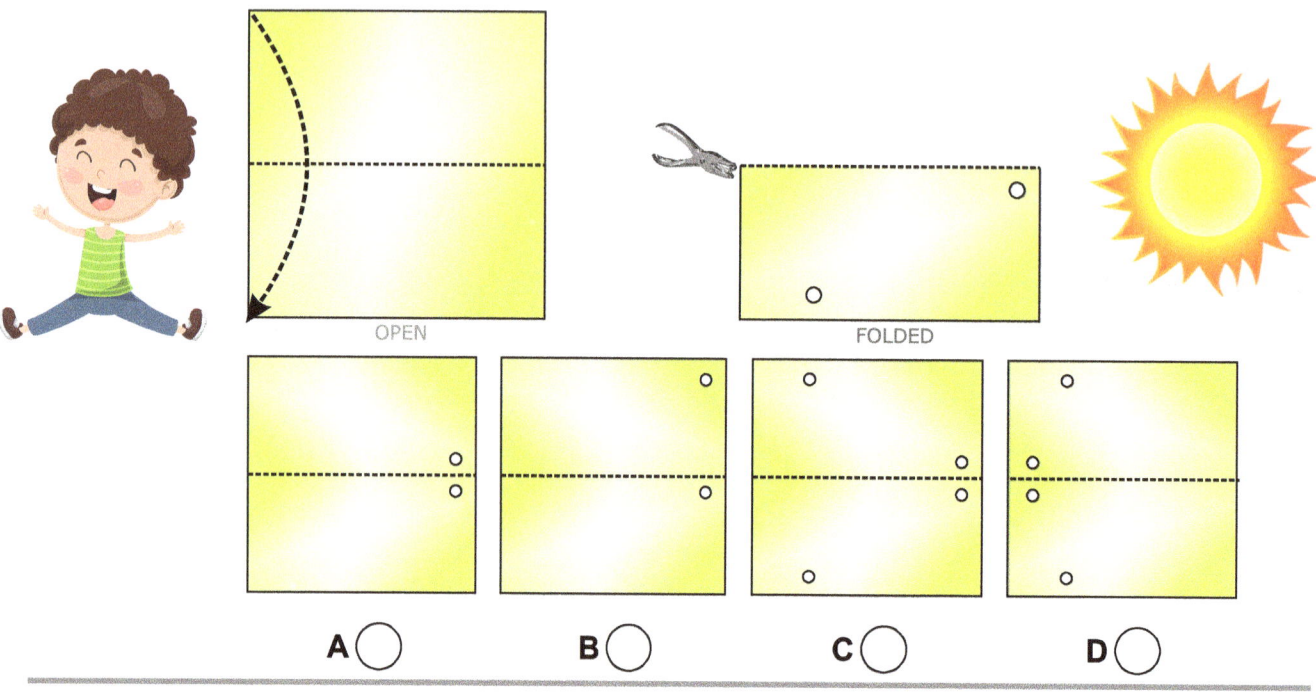

OPEN   FOLDED

A◯   B◯   C◯   D◯

Q-4

Look at the question and put your finger on Satellite. Emma folded the paper and made holes to it as shown. When the paper is unfolded how does it look? Help her bubble the right option.

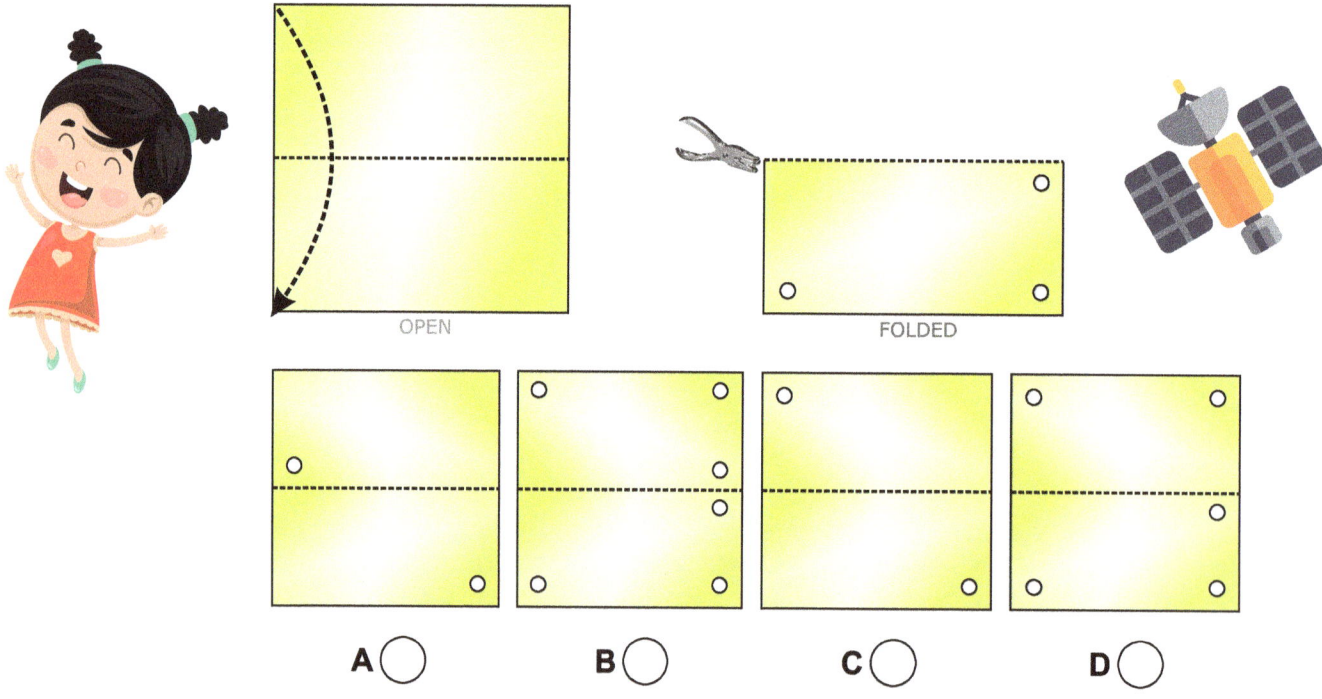

OPEN   FOLDED

A◯   B◯   C◯   D◯

©All rights reserved-Math-Knots LLC., VA-USA
www.math-knots.com

Q-5

Look at the question and put your finger on Rocket. Daniel folded the paper and made hole to it as shown. When the paper is unfolded how does it look? Help him bubble the right option.

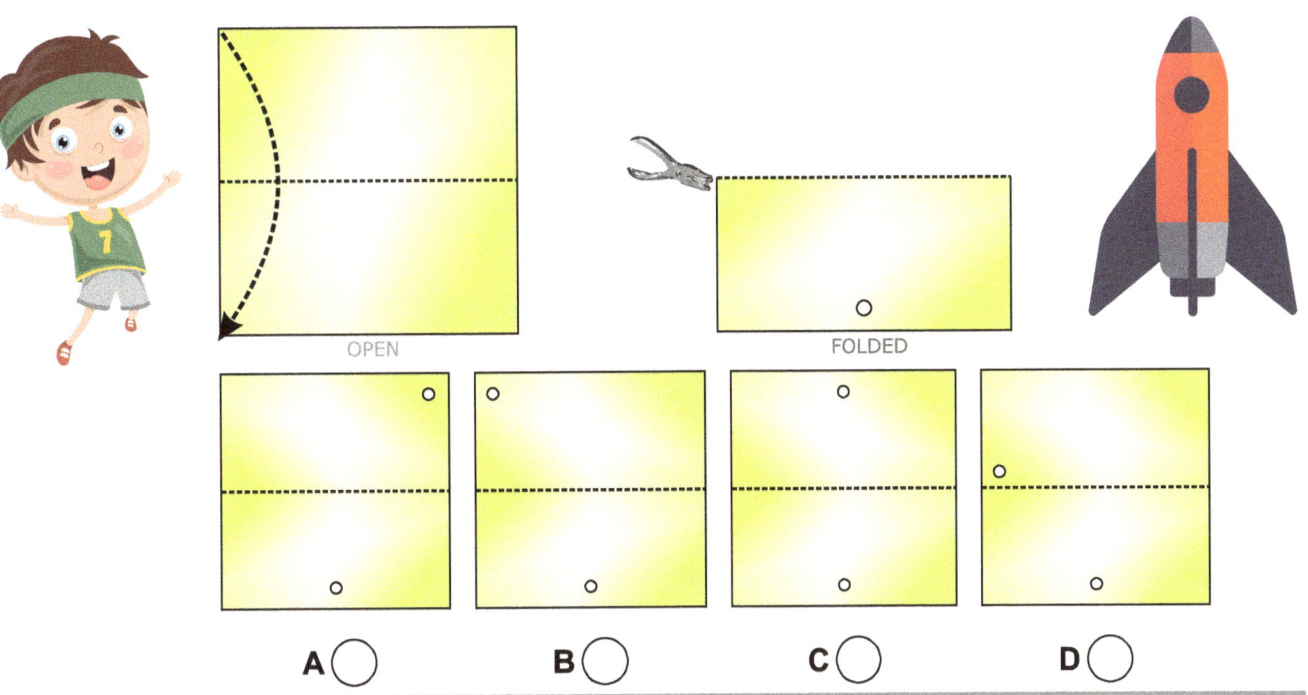

OPEN

FOLDED

A ◯   B ◯   C ◯   D ◯

Q-6

Look at the question and put your finger on Bulb. Emily folded the paper and made holes to it as shown. When the paper is unfolded how does it look? Help her bubble the right option.

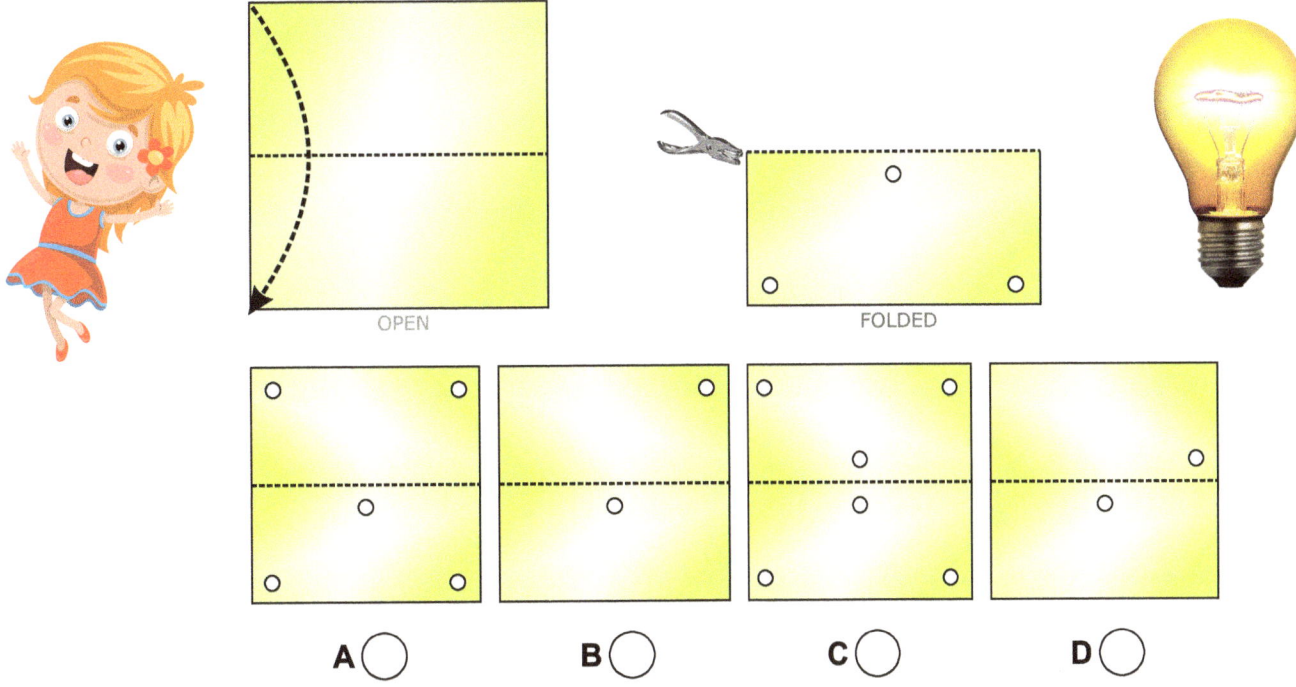

OPEN

FOLDED

A ◯   B ◯   C ◯   D ◯

©All rights reserved-Math-Knots LLC., VA-USA

www.math-knots.com

Q-7

Look at the question and put your finger on Satellite. Michael folded the paper and made holes to it as shown. When the paper is unfolded how does it look? Help him bubble the right option.

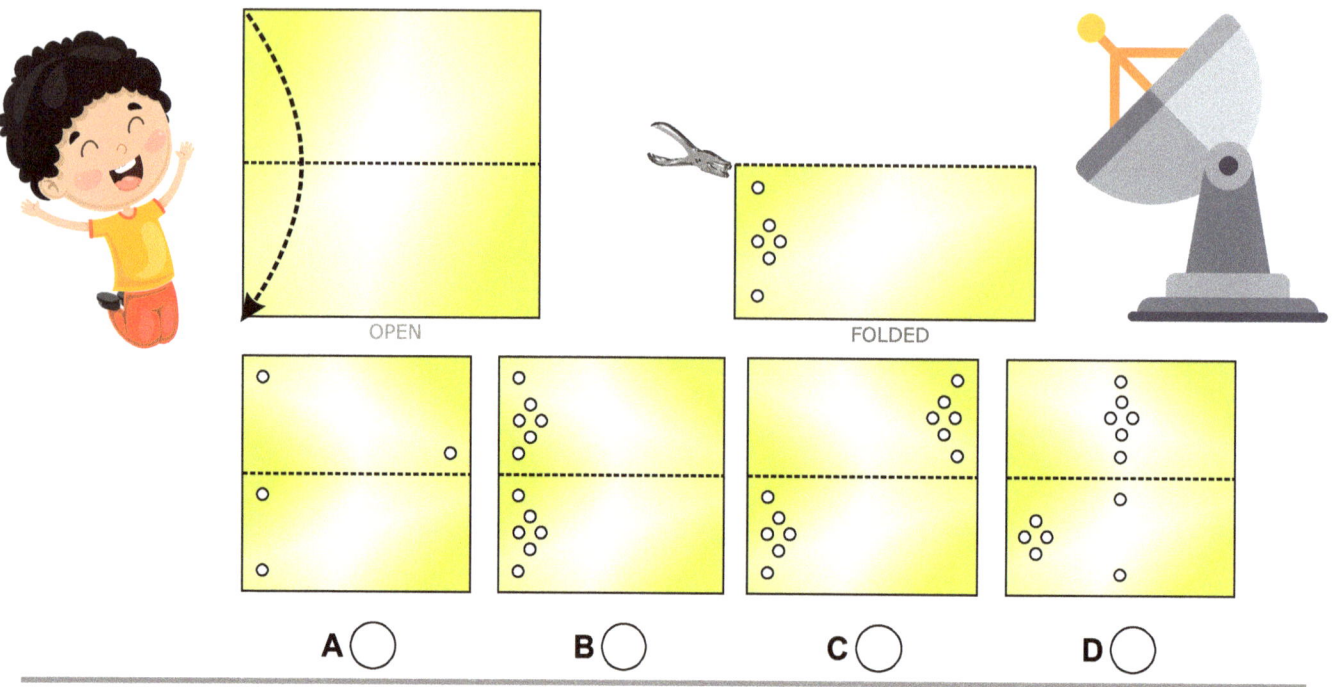

A ◯   B ◯   C ◯   D ◯

Q-8

Look at the question and put your finger on Telescope. Kathy folded the paper and made holes to it as shown. When the paper is unfolded how does it look? Help her bubble the right option.

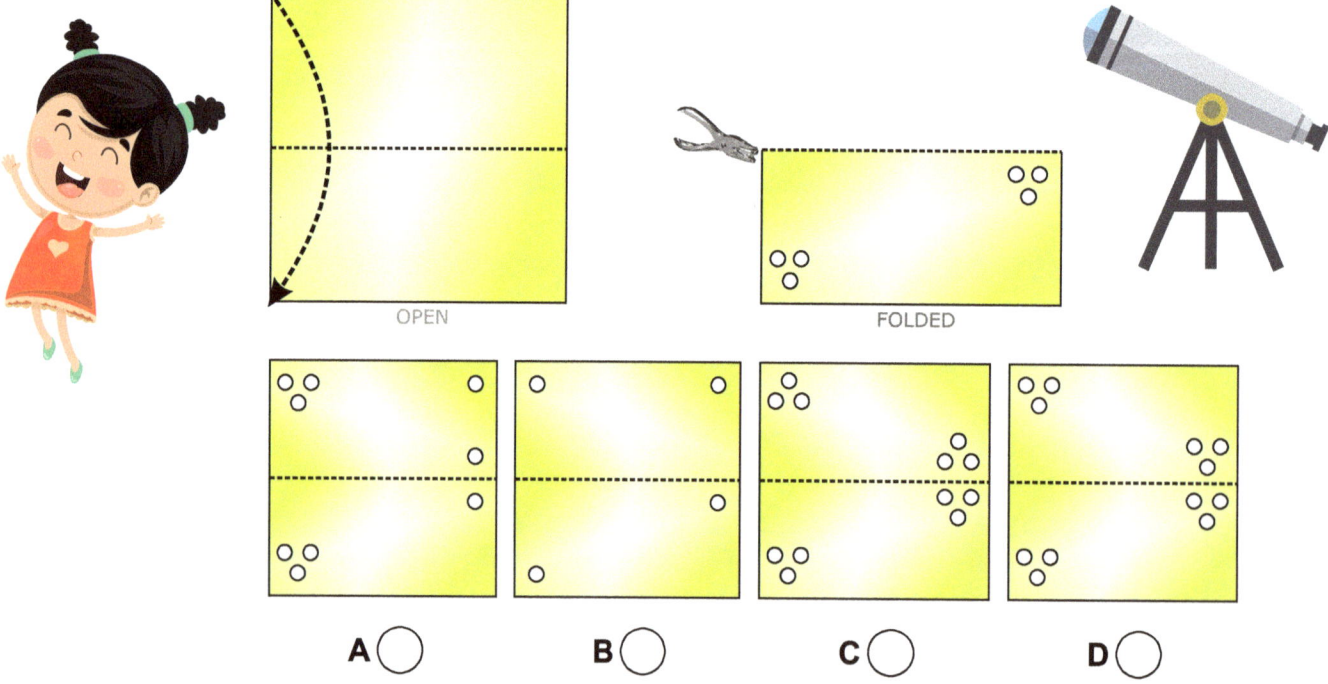

A ◯   B ◯   C ◯   D ◯

©All rights reserved-Math-Knots LLC., VA-USA

Q-9

Look at the question and put your finger on Globe. Madison folded the paper and made holes to it as shown. When the paper is unfolded how does it look? Help her bubble the right option.

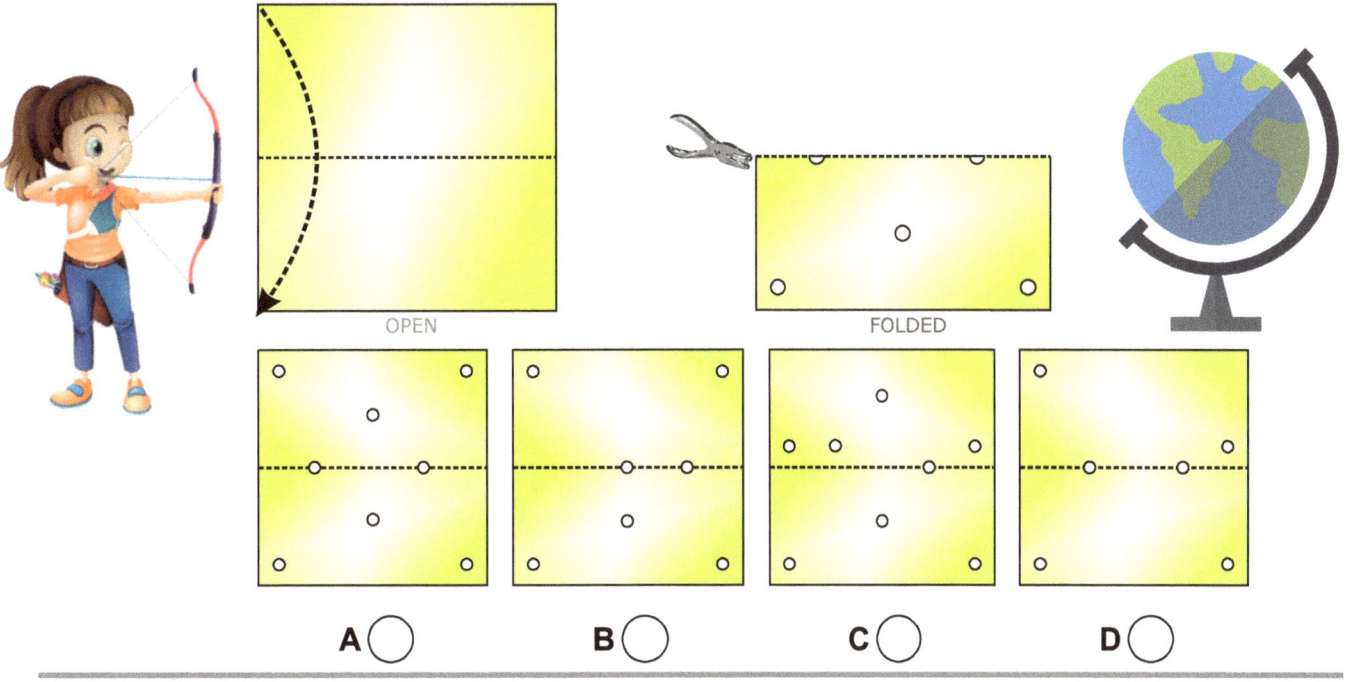

OPEN
FOLDED

A ◯   B ◯   C ◯   D ◯

Q-10

Look at the question and put your finger on Saturn. Ryan folded the paper and made holes to it as shown. When the paper is unfolded how does it look? Help him bubble the right option.

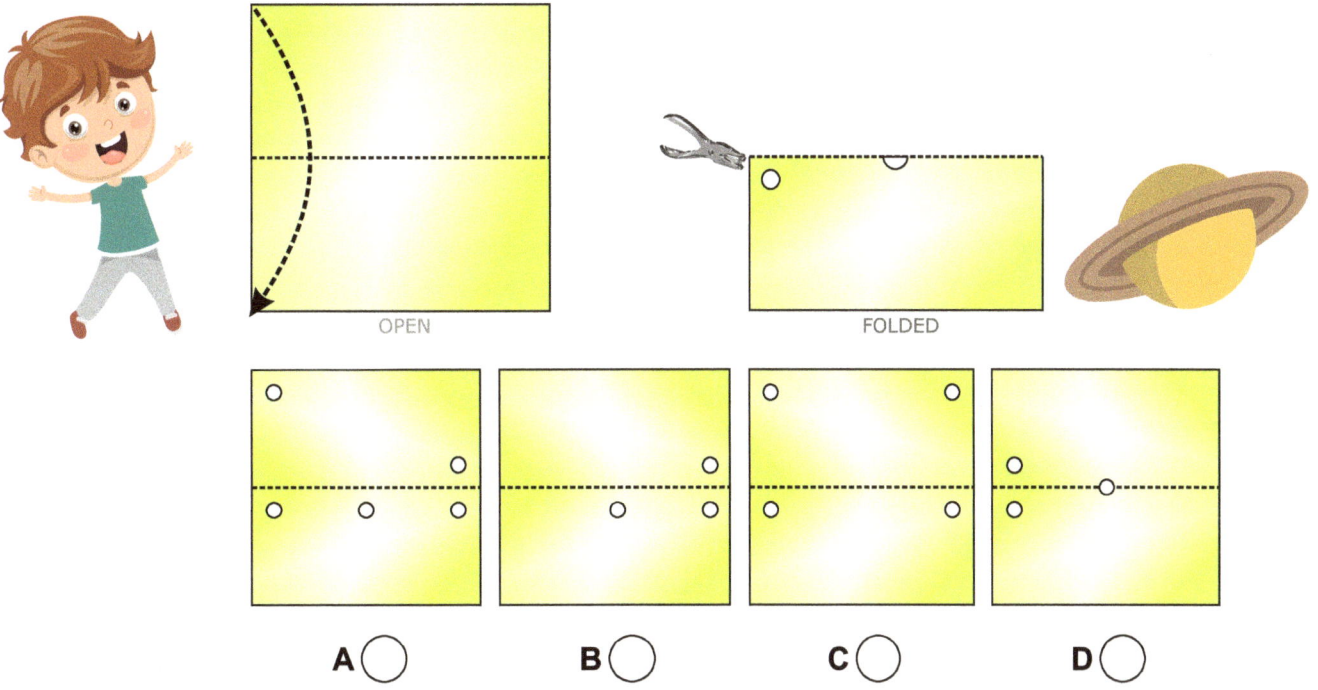

OPEN
FOLDED

A ◯   B ◯   C ◯   D ◯

©All rights reserved-Math-Knots LLC., VA-USA

www.math-knots.com

Q-11

Look at the question and put your finger on Thermometer. James folded the paper and made holes to it as shown. When the paper is unfolded how does it look? Help him bubble the right option.

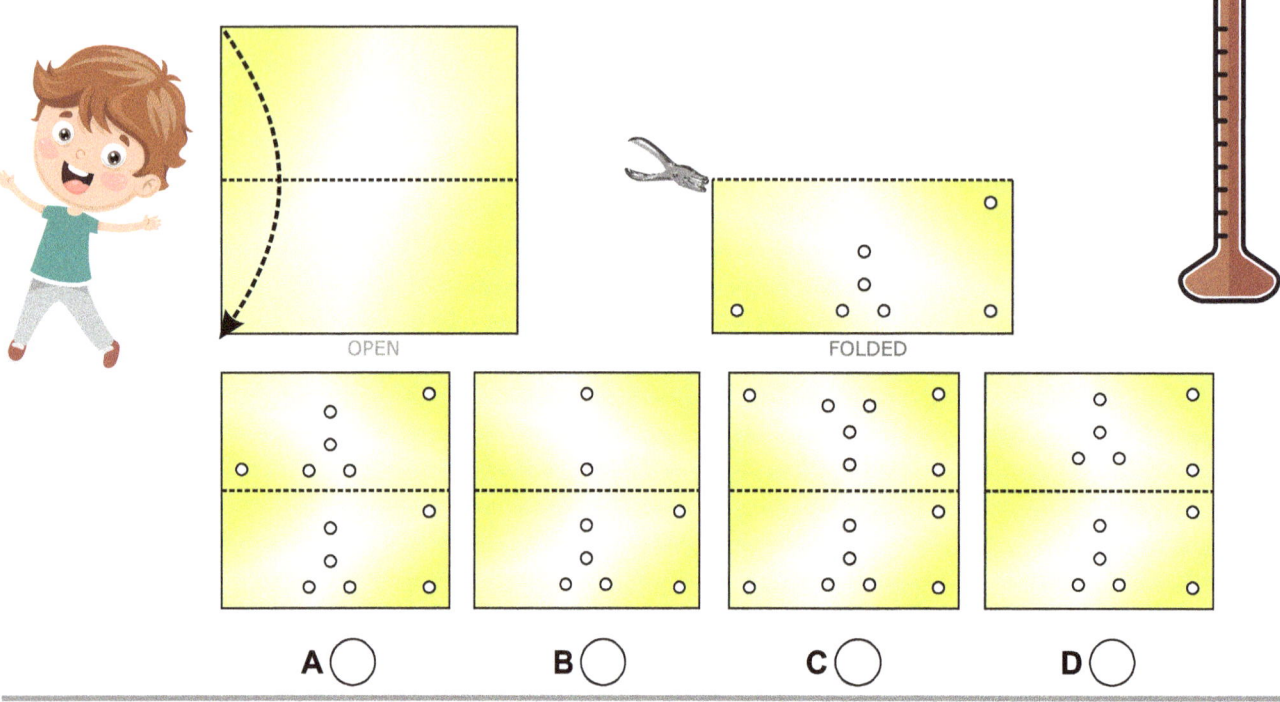

OPEN   FOLDED

A ◯   **B** ◯   **C** ◯   **D** ◯

Q-12

Look at the question and put your finger on Microscope. Olivia folded the paper and made holes to it as shown. When the paper is unfolded how does it look? Help her bubble the right option.

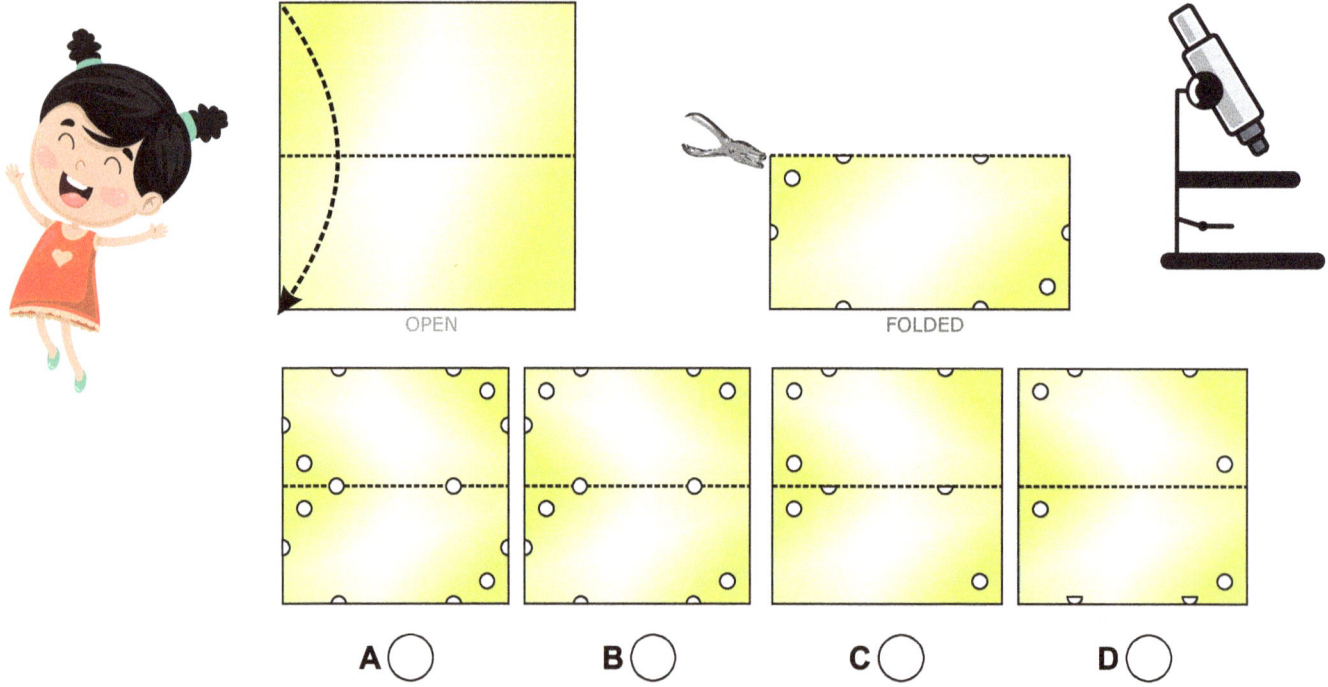

OPEN   FOLDED

A ◯   **B** ◯   **C** ◯   **D** ◯

©All rights reserved-Math-Knots LLC., VA-USA
www.math-knots.com

Q-13 Look at the question and put your finger on Magnet. Christopher folded the paper and made hole to it as shown. When the paper is unfolded how does it look? Help him bubble the right option.

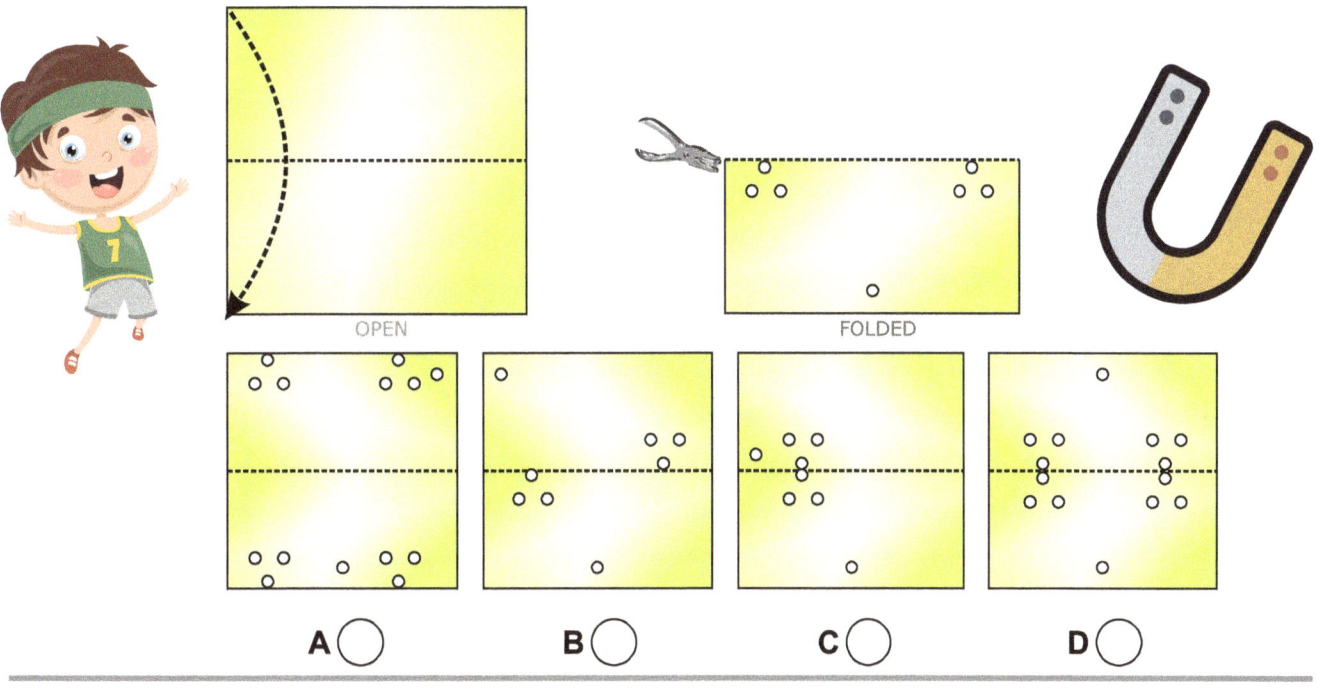

OPEN

FOLDED

A ⃝   B ⃝   C ⃝   D ⃝

Q-14 Look at the question and put your finger on Bearings. Emily folded the paper and made holes to it as shown. When the paper is unfolded how does it look? Help her bubble the right option.

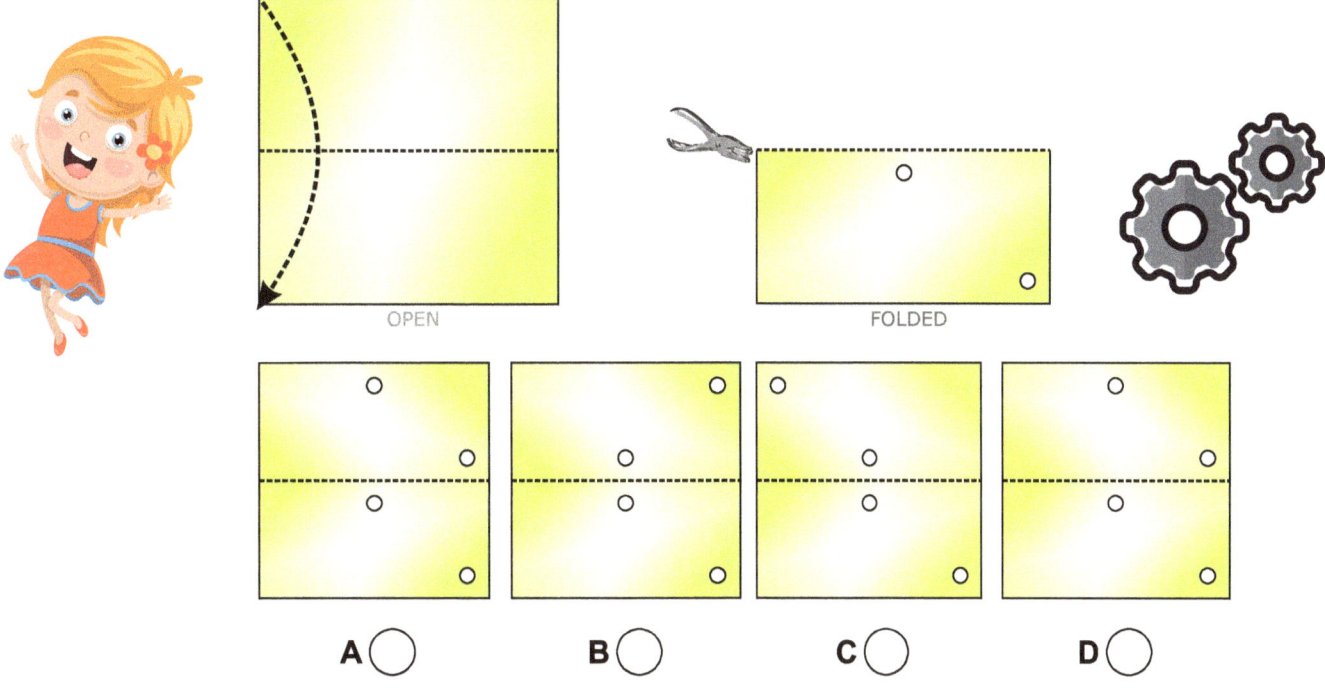

OPEN

FOLDED

A ⃝   B ⃝   C ⃝   D ⃝

©All rights reserved-Math-Knots LLC., VA-USA
www.math-knots.com

Q-15

Look at the question and put your finger on Galaxy. Mathew folded the paper and made hole to it as shown. When the paper is unfolded how does it look? Help him bubble the right option.

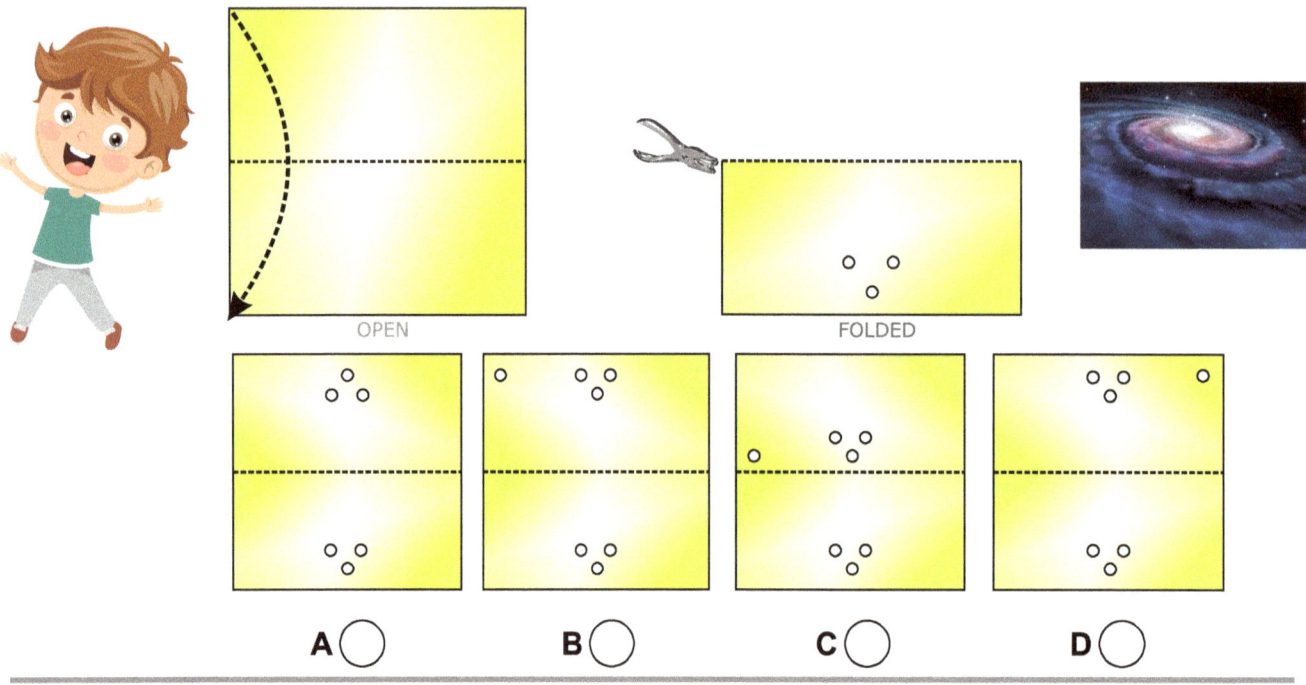

A ◯   B ◯   C ◯   D ◯

Q-16

Look at the question and put your finger on Clouds. Ashley folded the paper and made holes to it as shown. When the paper is unfolded how does it look? Help her bubble the right option.

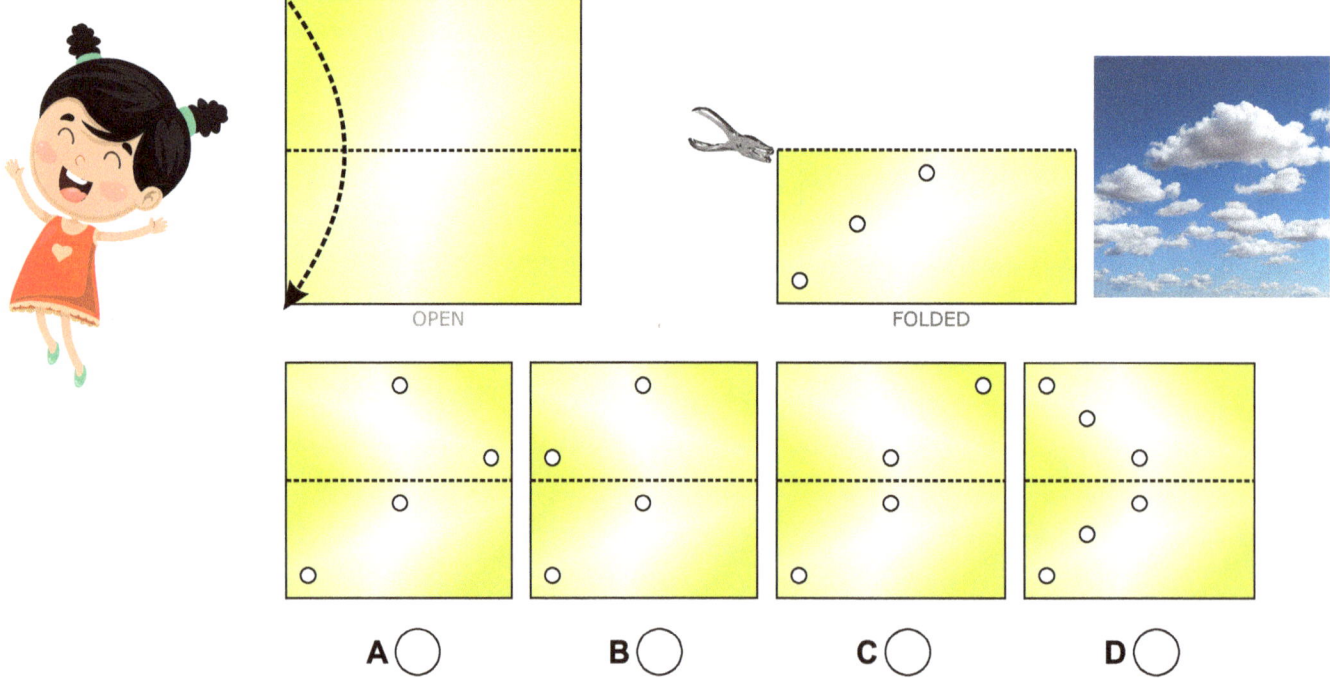

A ◯   B ◯   C ◯   D ◯

©All rights reserved-Math-Knots LLC., VA-USA

www.math-knots.com

MATH KNOT CHALLENGE

Q-17 Look at the question and put your finger on DNA. Tyler folded the paper and made holes to it as shown. When the paper is unfolded how does it look? Help him bubble the right option.

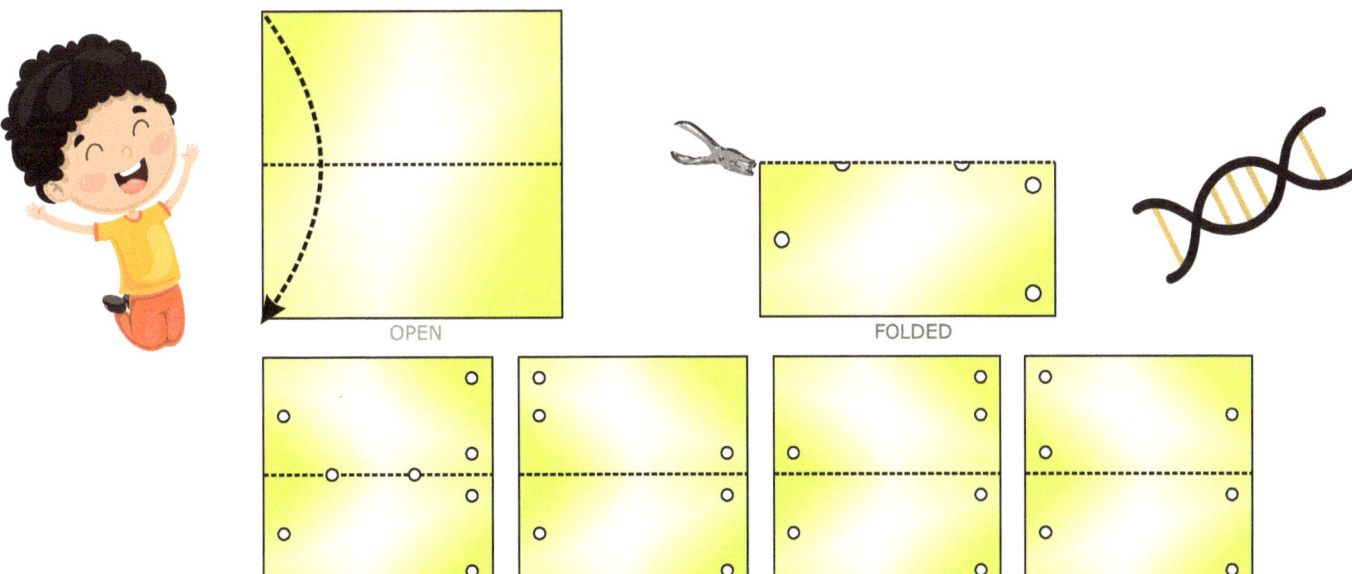

OPEN   FOLDED

A ◯   B ◯   C ◯   D ◯

MATH KNOT CHALLENGE

Q-18 Look at the question and put your finger on Cone. Alexis folded the paper and made holes to it as shown. When the paper is unfolded how does it look? Help her bubble the right option.

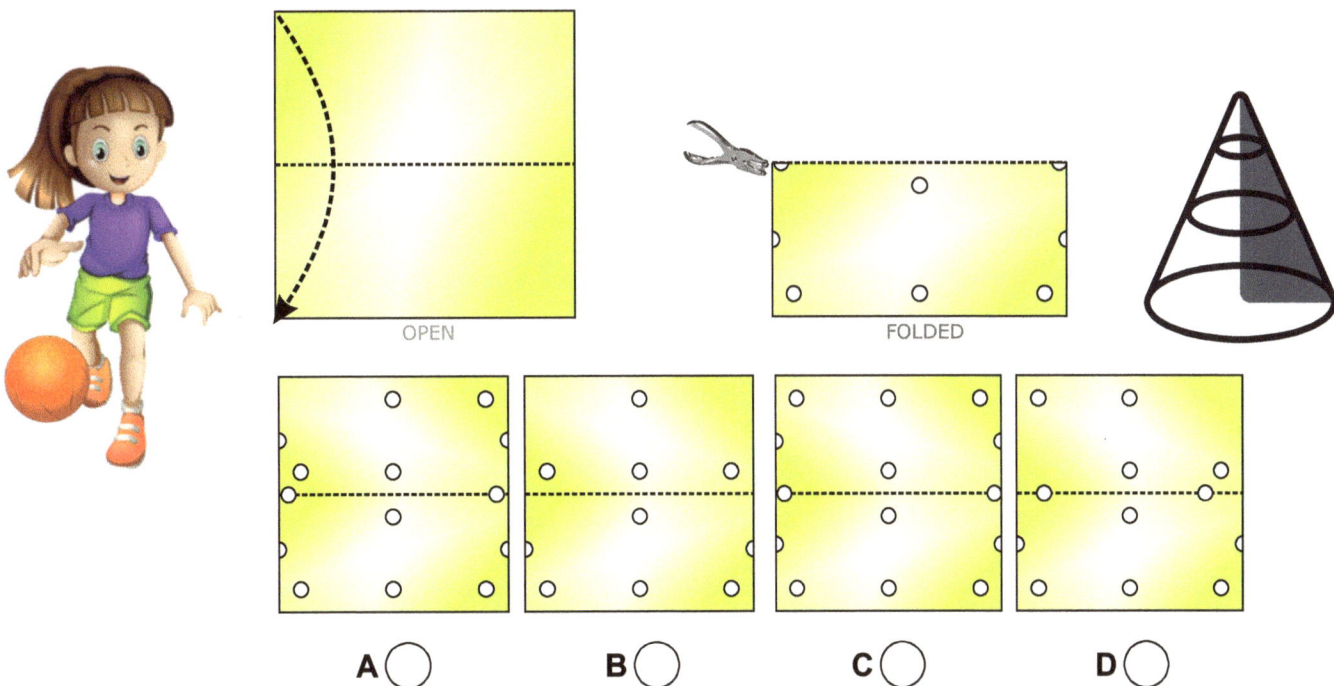

OPEN   FOLDED

A ◯   B ◯   C ◯   D ◯

©All rights reserved-Math-Knots LLC., VA-USA
www.math-knots.com

MATH KNOT CHALLENGE

Q-19

Look at the question and put your finger on Beakers. Joseph folded the paper and made holes to it as shown. When the paper is unfolded how does it look? Help him bubble the right option.

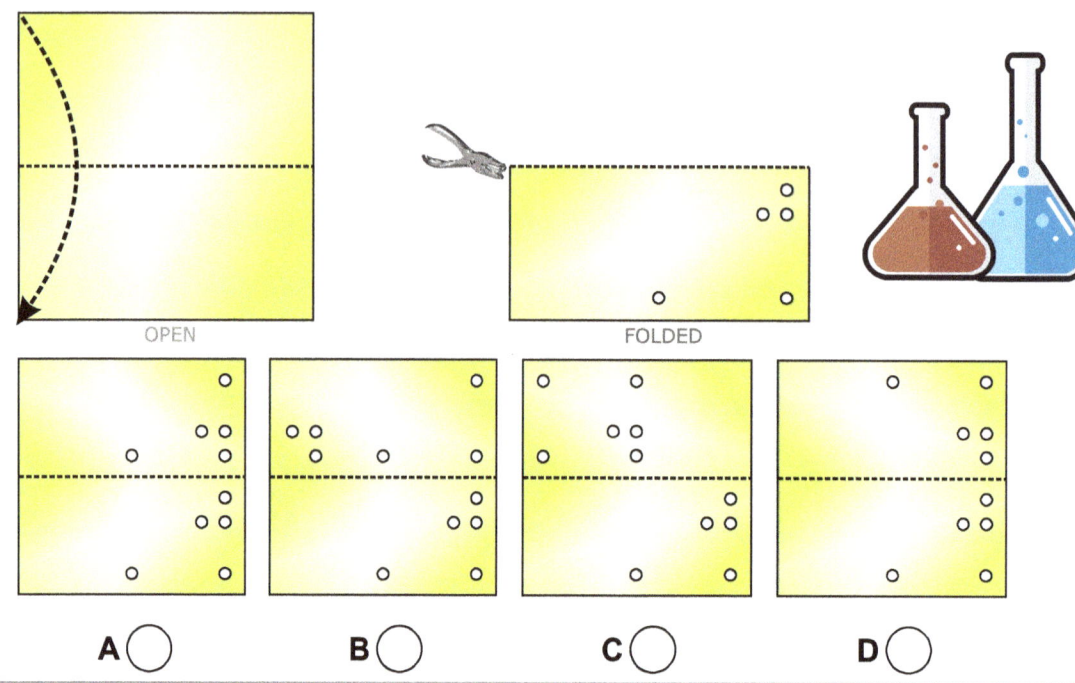

OPEN

FOLDED

A◯   B◯   C◯   D◯

MATH KNOT CHALLENGE

Q-20

Look at the question and put your finger on Safety Glasses. Sophia folded the paper and made holes to it as shown. When the paper is unfolded how does it look? Help her bubble the right option.

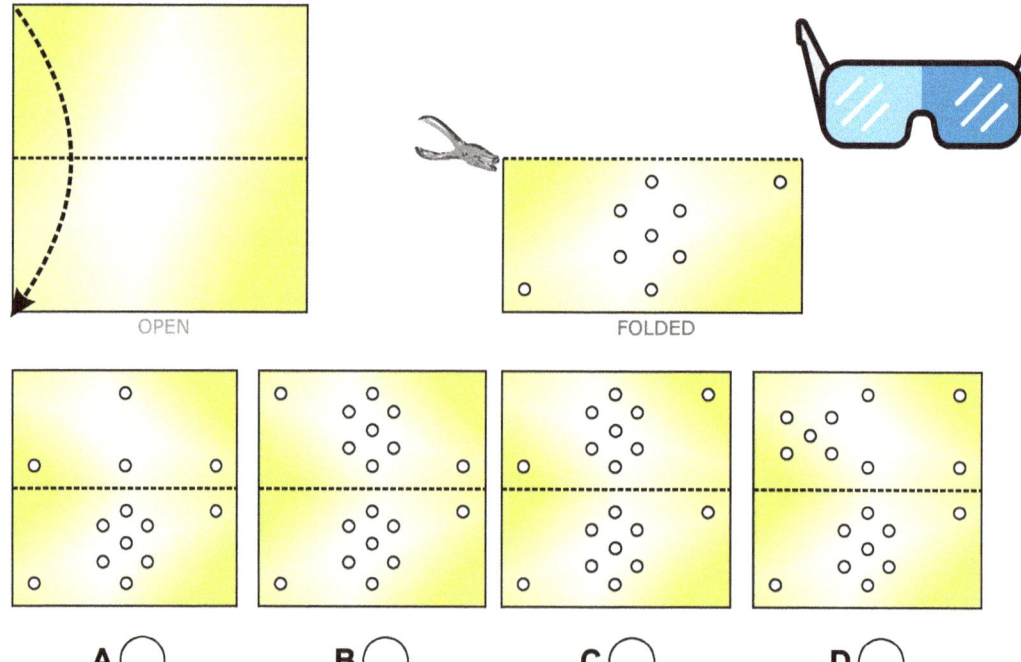

OPEN

FOLDED

A◯   B◯   C◯   D◯

©All rights reserved-Math-Knots LLC., VA-USA

www.math-knots.com

ANSWER KEYS

TEST - 1

Lets Start the Test...

©All rights reserved-Math-Knots LLC., VA-USA   131   www.math-knots.com

©All rights reserved-Math-Knots LLC., VA-USA

ANSWER KEY

1.   A ;   Types of things we wear or Garments

2.   A ;   All others are nature- bound, War is man-made

3.   C ;   All others are types of color

4.   D ;   All others are sense organs or related to sense organs

5.   B ;   Various types of gases

6.   D ;   Various expressions of joy

7.   A ;   Types of solid metals

8.   B ;   Various joints in human body

9.   D ;   Types of various professions

10. C ;   Various types of instructors

11. B ;   Various types of string instruments

12. B ;   Various forms of running water

13. D ;   Parts of tree above ground

14. A ;   Various types of transportations

15. C ;   Types of players in various sports

16. D ;   Permission meanings

17. B ;   Things made of wood

18. A ;   Meanings of highest point

©All rights reserved-Math-Knots LLC., VA-USA   **133**

ANSWER KEY

1.   A

As the wind Blows tent is pushed aside

2.   C

Fastest way of transportation is Aero plane

3.   B

A boat is used to cross the river

4.   A

To shop we need money and money is kept in hand bag.
Out of the given choices hand bag is the right option to choose

5.   D

Rita needs to dress up warmly to play in snow, otherwise she
will fall sick. Option D shows winter hat and gloves

6.   B

Enclosed means surround or close off on all sides. Picture is
closed by frame Circle is closed by star. Map is enclosing the
area. Option B, the letter U is not surrounding anything and
has an opening on the top

7.   A

Single means one. Option A, showing a Baby is the single kid

8.   D

Option D is showing all 9 planets

9.   A

Lion and cat can't fly. Dolphins swim and jump but don't fly.
Aero plane is the only one which flies

ANSWER KEY

10. C

A pair means two. Three pairs of objects mean six objects in total

11. A

Carl needs an electric socket to charge his cellphone and laptop

12. D

Hair band is some thing that girls use to decorate their hair on the head

13. B

Pack means a group of wild animals like wolves, tigers etc....
Pack is also a box and the items within it

14. C

Option C, Ranch is a common tool found in tool box

15. A

Croak sounds are made by Frogs

16. D

Sriyan can't open the laptop as he is too young

17. D

Violin / Viola / Guitar all belong to strings family of instruments

18. B

From the given options Red Car is the right choice. It same of the same color as tomato

©All rights reserved-Math-Knots LLC., VA-USA

www.math-knots.com

ANSWER KEY

1.   A

2.   D

3.   C

4.   D

5.   A

6.   C

7.   A

8.   D

9.   C

10.   B

11.   D

12.   A

13.   C

14.   B

15.   D

16.   B

17.   C

18.   A

©All rights reserved-Math-Knots LLC., VA-USA
www.math-knots.com

ANSWER KEY

1.   A

   1 --> 4 (Add 3)

   1 --> 4 (Add 3)

2.   D

   6 --> 3 (Half)

   10 --> 5 (Half)

3.   C

   4 --> 4 (Same count of objects)

   6 --> 6 (Same count of objects)

4.   A

   3 --> 6 (Double)

   2 --> 4 (Double)

5.   B

   3 --> 4 (Add 1)

   6 --> 7 (Add 1)

6.   D

   5 --> 10 (Double)

   6 --> 12 (Double)

7.   A

   4 --> 3 (Subtract 1)

   5 --> 4 (Subtract 1)

©All rights reserved-Math-Knots LLC., VA-USA
www.math-knots.com

ANSWER KEY

8.   B

   7 --> 5 (Subtract 2)

   9 --> 7 (Subtract 2)

9.   A

   1 --> 5 (Add 4)

   2 --> 6 (Add 4)

10.   C

   1 --> 7 (Add 6)

   1 --> 7 (Add 6)

11.   D

   1 --> 6 (Add 5)

   1 --> 6 (Add 5)

12.   A

   8 --> 1 (Subtract 7)

   8 --> 1 (Subtract 7)

13.   D

   1 --> 2 (Add 1)

   1 --> 2 (Add 1)

14.   D

   2 --> 5 (Add 3)

   5 --> 8 (Add 3)

©All rights reserved-Math-Knots LLC., VA-USA

ANSWER KEY

15.   B

    8 --> 4 (Half)

    4 --> 2 (Half)

16.   C

    One wheel --> 2 wheels per object

    Two wheels --> 4 wheels object

17.   A

    Half --> Full (Double / Twice)

    2 --> 4 (Double /Twice)

18.   D

    1 whole Pizza --> One slice

    1 Whole cake --> One slice

ANSWER KEY

1. A

    6, 4, 2, 0 ; Numbers are decreasing by 2

2. D

    2, 2, 3, 3, 4, 4 ; Each number is repeating twice and then increasing by 1

3. D

    5, 5, 3, ?, 5, 5; Each number is repeating twice and decreasing by 2 So, answer is 5, 5, 3, 3, 5, 5

4. B

    1, 5, 1, 5, 1, 5; 1 and 5 are repeating

5. C

    8, 6, 4, 2 ; Numbers are decreasing by 2

6. A

    4, 3, 3, 2, 2, 1; Alternate numbers are decreasing by 1
    4, 3, 2 are one group & 3, 2, 1 are another group

7. C

    5, 0, 0, 5, 0, 0, 5; 5, 0, 0 is the repeating sequence

8. D

    0, 2, 4, 6, 8; Increasing by two

9. A

    0, 7, 0, 7, 0, 7; Repeating sequence of 0 and 7

10. C

    4, 5, 3, 4, 2, 3; Alternate numbers are decreasing by 1
    4, 3, 2 are one group & 5, 4, 3 are another group

©All rights reserved-Math-Knots LLC., VA-USA
www.math-knots.com

ANSWER KEY

11.   B

5, 3, 1, 5, 3, 1; Repeating sequence of 5, 3 and 1

12.   D

0, 0, 6, 0, 0, 6; Repeating sequence of 0, 0 and 6

13.   A

4, 4, 3, 5, 2, 6; Alternate numbers are decreasing by 1
Alternate numbers are increasing by 1.
5, 3, 2 are one group & 4, 5, 6 are one group

14.   C

7, 6, 5, 7, 6, 5; Repeating sequence of 7, 6 and 5

15.   D

5, 4, 3, 2, 1; Numbers are decreasing by 1

16.   C

2, 2, 4, 4, 2, 2, 4; Repeating sequence of 2, 2, 4, 4 and
then 2, 2, 4, 4

17.   A

11, 9, 9, 11, 7 Alternate numbers are decreasing by 2
Alternate numbers are increasing by 2
11, 9, 7 are one group & 9, 11, 13 are one group

18.   B

1, 2, 2, 3, 3, 4; Alternate numbers are increasing by 1

ANSWER KEY

1.   B

$1 + 6 = 7$

2.   A

$3 + 5 = 8$

3.   C

$6 + 4 = 10$

4.   D

$2 + 6 = 8$

5.   B

$4 + 4 = 8$

6.   A

$1 + 3 = 4$

7.   B

$6 + 3 = 9$

8.   D

$4 + 6 + 4 = 14$

9.   A

$9 + 4 + 1 = 13 + 1 = 14$

10.   C

$2 + 5 + 3 = 7 + 3 = 10$

©All rights reserved-Math-Knots LLC., VA-USA
www.math-knots.com

ANSWER KEY

11. C

$$5 + 1 + 7 = 6 + 7 = 13$$

12. D

$$2 + 4 + 6 = 12$$

13. B

$$6 + 1 + 9 = 16$$

14. B

$$10 + 0 + 0 = 10$$

15. A

$$9 - 4 + 1 = 5 + 1 = 6$$

16. D

$$2 + 5 - 3 = 7 - 3 = 4$$

17. C

$$4 + 1 - 2 = 5 - 2 = 3$$

18. D

$$6 + 5 + 0 = 11$$

19. A

$$6 + 1 + 9 = 7 + 9 = 16$$

20. B

$$5 + 3 + 1 = 9$$

©All rights reserved-Math-Knots LLC., VA-USA

ANSWER KEY

1.	A	Figures are turning 90 degrees. The best option is A
2.	A	Three figures are overlapping
3.	D	One flower with 5 petals
4.	B	Three curves cutting the circle
5.	C	Two lines cutting in the rectangle. Red line on top of green line
6.	A	Only option A matches to the group with two stars, two circles and 7 lines
7.	B	Only picture with & ,%,@ and # in sequence is option B in
8.	D	Only option with ? , @ and X
9.	C	Only option with green half circles at one end
10.	B	Only option B has # in the center and towards ends

©All rights reserved-Math-Knots LLC., VA-USA

www.math-knots.com

ANSWER KEY

11.	D	All three triangles are rotated together
12.	C	Green half circle has horizontal lines. Blue half circle has vertical lines
13.	A	Alphabet between two consecutive even numbers
14.	B	Two same alphabet
15.	C	Three dots in one line with closed end. Two dots in one line with open end
16.	B	Five lines originating from the same point with circles at the end
17.	A	Two stars and three triangles
18.	D	Four red circles with yellow circle on top. Looks like a flower

©All rights reserved-Math-Knots LLC., VA-USA
www.math-knots.com

ANSWER KEY

1.   A

Angle to straight figure

2.   D

Turning 90° to right side

3.   C

Turning 90° to right side and flipping right to left.

4.   A

Flipping up to down

5.   B

Lines to checks

6.   D

One turn 90° with same petals

7.   C

Dashed lines are connecting and filling the figure

8.   C

Outside symbols on the triangle are turning anti clock wise one turn

9.   A

4 sides to 5 sides. Number sides are increasing, so 5 sides to six sides

10.   D

Dots and checks interchange in first row

Stars and checks interchange for the second row

ANSWER KEY

11.   C

Flipping up and down

12.   D

First row: First picture has only circles. Second Picture
has two symbols (one additional)
The first picture in second row should have circles

13.   A

Size is decreasing

14.   C

First Row first picture to second picture: Flipping of top
figure in first one gives second picture of first row

15.   B

Figures in between two rays or pointed objects are moving
three slots

16.   D

Picture filled and shown transparently with shapes

17.   A

Moon inside the circle is moved to outside. So, Triangle inside
Trapezium is moved outside

18.   A

First figure above the line is moving down, while the figure
below the line is moving inside the second figure above the line

ANSWER KEY

1.   A ;

2.   D ;

3.   C ;

4.   B ;

5.   C ;

6.   C ;

7.   B ;

8.   C ;

9.   A ;

10.   D ;

11.   C;

12.   A;

13.   D;

14.   B;

15.   A;

16.   D;

BONUS CHALLENGE QUESTIONS

17.   A ;

18.   C ;

19.   D ;

20.   B ;

©All rights reserved-Math-Knots LLC., VA-USA

www.math-knots.com

- We have provided 16 paper folded and punched final figures.

- These pages can be tored, pictures can be cut. Student can fold the pictures along the line and understand the concept.

- This will help them in understanding their visualization of the figures.

©All rights reserved-Math-Knots LLC., VA-USA

www.math-knots.com

©All rights reserved-Math-Knots LLC., VA-USA

Q1

Q2

Q3

Q4

Q5

Q6

Q7

Q8

©All rights reserved-Math-Knots LLC., VA-USA

Q9

Q13

Q10

Q14

Q11

Q15

Q12

Q16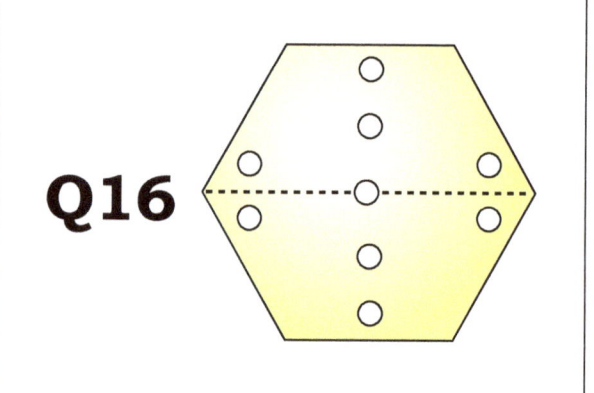

©All rights reserved-Math-Knots LLC., VA-USA

www.math-knots.com

	A	B	C	D
Q1.	○	○	○	○
Q2.	○	○	○	○
Q3.	○	○	○	○
Q4.	○	○	○	○
Q5.	○	○	○	○
Q6.	○	○	○	○
Q7.	○	○	○	○
Q8.	○	○	○	○
Q9.	○	○	○	○
Q10.	○	○	○	○
Q11.	○	○	○	○
Q12.	○	○	○	○
Q13.	○	○	○	○
Q14.	○	○	○	○
Q15.	○	○	○	○
Q16.	○	○	○	○
Q17.	○	○	○	○
Q 18.	○	○	○	○
Q 19.	○	○	○	○
Q 20.	○	○	○	○

©All rights reserved-Math-Knots LLC., VA-USA

www.math-knots.com

©All rights reserved-Math-Knots LLC., VA-USA

www.ingramcontent.com/pod-product-compliance
Lightning Source LLC
Chambersburg PA
CBHW052143140626

46547CB00039B/2730